Presented To:

Dave & Becky

From:

Date:

D0612258

A Practical Guide to Evangelism— Supernaturally

Dave & Becky

A Practical Guide to Evangelism— Supernaturally

CHRIS OVERSTREET

© Copyright 2011—Chris Overstreet

All rights reserved. This book is protected by the copyright laws of the United States of America. This book may not be copied or reprinted for commercial gain or profit. The use of short quotations or occasional page copying for personal or group study is permitted and encouraged. Permission will be granted upon request. Unless otherwise identified, Scripture quotations are taken from the New King James Version. Copyright © 1982 by Thomas Nelson, Inc. Used by permission. All rights reserved. Scripture quotations marked NIV are taken from the HOLY BIBLE, NEW INTERNATIONAL VERSION®, Copyright © 1973, 1978, 1984 International Bible Society. Used by permission of Zondervan. All rights reserved. Scripture quotations marked KJV are taken from the King James Version. Scripture quotations marked NASB are taken from the NEW AMERICAN STANDARD BIBLE®, Copyright © 1960,1962,1963, 1968,1971,1972,1973,1975,1977,1995 by The Lockman Foundation. Used by permission. Please note that Destiny Image's publishing style capitalizes certain pronouns in Scripture that refer to the Father, Son, and Holy Spirit, and may differ from some publishers' styles. Take note that the name satan and related names are not capitalized. We choose not to acknowledge him, even to the point of violating grammatical rules.

DESTINY IMAGE® PUBLISHERS, INC.

P.O. Box 310, Shippensburg, PA 17257-0310

"Speaking to the Purposes of God for This Generation and for the Generations to Come."

This book and all other Destiny Image, Revival Press, MercyPlace, Fresh Bread, Destiny Image Fiction, and Treasure House books are available at Christian bookstores and distributors worldwide.

For a U.S. bookstore nearest you, call 1-800-722-6774.

For more information on foreign distributors, call 717-532-3040.

Reach us on the Internet: www.destinyimage.com.

ISBN 13 TP: 978-0-7684-3827-7
ISBN 13 HC: 978-0-7684-3828-4
ISBN 13 LP: 978-0-7684-3829-1
ISBN 13 Ebook: 978-0-7684-8980-4

For Worldwide Distribution, Printed in the U.S.A.

4 5 6 7 8 9 10 11 / 13

Dedication

I want to dedicate this book and all of its proceeds to the Heroes of the Nation in Kenya, Africa.

In 2006, I met with Andrew Sievright, president of Heroes of the Nation (HTN), over a cup of coffee. As we talked, he shared that he wanted to send me to Kenya because he had seen a vision of me loving the people there and being loved by the people there. I went to Kenya that summer with a team from Bethel Church, Redding, California, and saw the beautiful children for myself. I realized on that trip that these children are not orphans, but that they are truly *heroes*. I knew from that moment on that I would be forever connected with this ministry and their vision to train and equip orphans to be the heroes of their nations.

When you buy this book, you are not only going to be equipped for evangelism, but you are making a difference in the lives of children in Africa.

For more information about Heroes of the Nation in Kenya, Africa, please visit www.HTN.org

Acknowledgments

I want to thank my wife, Stefanie, my love and ministry partner, for believing in me and dreaming with me to touch the world with the love and power of God.

I also want to thank Bill Johnson and Kris Vallotton and all my spiritual fathers and mothers for pouring into me and investing in my life throughout the years. This book could never have been written apart from your help.

I also want to thank Christina Files, who helped to edit this book. Thanks, also, to Destiny Image, who designed my cover.

Lastly, I want to thank Aaron McMahon for approaching me and encouraging me to write this book. Aaron, a graduate of Bethel School of Supernatural Ministry, met with me for over a year to help me process my thoughts and get them out on paper. I highly recommend his book, *How to Write & Publish Your Book*, as it practically teaches you how to make the dream of writing a book a reality. Aaron's book is available at his website: www.aaronmcmahon.com. Thanks again, bro!

Endorsements

A lot of modern evangelism has become a highly developed form of manipulation, where lost people become projects; their prayers counted as scores in some kind of strange game where the real goal seems to be winning favor with God.

Chris Overstreet's *A Practical Guide to Evangelism—Supernaturally* has captured God's heart for undefiled, childlike ministry to the lost. This book was born out of Chris's own experience. He has been loving the lost into the Kingdom in our community for nearly a decade. His encounters with unbelievers can only be described as supernaturally inspired, Holy Spirit journeys into the very heart of people. Several years ago, Chris started teaching, training, and deploying our ministry students to reach the lost. The fruit has been amazing. Every week hundreds of people, in the darkest places in our city, are touched with the love of Jesus. Even the bars in our community welcome our teams into their businesses to bless their patrons. Every day the reports come in of people being healed, set free from addictions, and saved.

This book is not just another book about "how to win friends and influence people." No, this book is a shepherd's guide to wooing wayward sheep back into the flock. Our Heavenly Father is waiting eagerly in His field of dreams, watching expectantly for His prodigals to return from the pig farm of poverty to the palace of purity. Chris shows us how to stand by His side to welcome them home. Supernatural evangelism could change your life—but more importantly, this book could be a catalyst to a global revival, which facilitates the greatest harvest of souls in all of history. Study this book and join the revolution!

KRIS VALLOTTON
Senior Associate Leader, Bethel Church, Redding, California
Co-Founder, Bethel School of Supernatural Ministry
Author of *The Supernatural Ways of Royalty*

A Practical Guide to Evangelism—Supernaturally is a must read for all those desiring to be activated in evangelism. The Bible tells us that God is *"not willing that any should perish"* (2 Pet. 3:9). God's heart is burning for those who do not know His radical love and He is calling His people to demonstrate His love and power to a lost and dying world. Chris Overstreet is one who has responded to that call and whose passion for the lost is evident to all those around him. Chris writes not from a place of theory but from real-life experience birthed out of a heart for God and those who have yet to experience the saving grace of God. The grace on Chris's life to equip and activate the Body of Christ has born fruit not only in the community of Bethel Church but all over the world. The teachings in *A Practical Guide to Evangelism— Supernaturally* will release a grace in your life to see God's desires fulfilled as the lost are found, the broken are made whole, and the lonely are put in a family.

BANNING LIEBSCHER
Director of Jesus Culture
at Bethel Church, Redding, California
Author of *Jesus Culture*

This book will help put you on the crest of the next wave of God....His power flowing through *you* everywhere you go! The people of God may be confident that miracles can flow in church meetings but are still timid when we are around non-Christians. We need these simple truths *deeply!* The chapter on fear is worth the price of the whole book! It is time to rise up with the spirit of David and take down the enemy with the love of Jesus and the power of the Holy Spirit.

TOM RUOTOLO
Founder of Power and Love Ministries
www.Powerandlove.org

I have had the pleasure of knowing Chris Overstreet for eight years. In that time, I have watched his passion, commitment, and dedication to evangelize the lost never wane, but only increase.

It is one thing to want to save souls, it's another thing to be taught the process by one who has a fiery call to the "office" of evangelist and radiates Heaven's passion for the lost. Chris Overstreet is one of those rare individuals. I love Chris for his pure motives, his sincere love for the common man, and his desire to win them to Christ, but I love him most because of his beautiful and humble heart. That kind of heart allows him to "receive" from Heaven such wealth of Spirit and revelation. This book is the fruit of this "revelation" that Chris not only receives but also lives out. In my 42 years of being a Christian, *A Practical Guide to Evangelism—Supernaturally* is the most powerful evangelism book I have ever read. Chris makes "winning the lost" as natural as breathing. This is a book of fiery motivation and deep self-discovery. Strap on your seatbelt, it's going to be a life-changing ride!

ANDREW SIEVRIGHT
President, Heroes of the Nation
www.HTN.org

This is a great book! It is powerful and practical. Every Christian should read this book.

STEVE BACKLUND
Bethel Church/Global Legacy

I'm always excited to see a *vessel* rise up to equip God's Army with both *revelation and relevance,* insight and instructions, and with experience and exploits. Chris Overstreet's book is all of the above. Recently, I got a chance to pray and witness at a health club as God touched a lady's neck that was seriously immobile and got to see God heal her on the spot. I was thinking what an impact that it had and still has on this lady. These types of miracles are waiting to be unlocked everyday, if we could be Holy Ghost CSI agents, who had an eye for the *fingerprints* of God in everyday life. Chris has that eye and shows you how to get it. *A Practical Guide to Evangelism—Supernaturally* is exactly what we rank-and-file believers need to step out into the miraculous dimension in the marketplace. This book will give you very practical steps to both step into the Spirit and step out into the streets to see signs and wonders released. In these pages are instructions that will bring Heaven to bear upon the life of the un-won. Chris brings a down-to-earth approach, that also brings Heaven with it. From beginning to end, get ready to be launched into a new dimension of the supernatural and a new release in the Gifts. I highly recommend this work to the entire Body of Christ to prepare us for the *Next Great Awakening* and your part in it!

SEAN SMITH

Author of *Prophetic Evangelism*

I first met Chris Overstreet when I filmed with him for my first movie, *Finger of God*. It was one of the more comical moments for this conservative, skeptical filmmaker to go out to dinner, or coffee, or anywhere really, with Chris and literally have to wait around most of the time because the guy kept stopping every other second to pray for perfect strangers. At first, I chuckled nervously at his audacity, but I soon found myself looking forward to the next one because it meant I'd get to see God touch another life. I also remember thinking how easy he made it all look. Well, now Chris has written *A Practical Guide to Evangelism—Supernaturally,* and in it he shows that supernatural evangelism actually is easy. This book is about as easy of a read as you can get, and you can't help but walk away from this thing thinking, "Man, even I can do that!" What I've always loved about Chris is that he is a guy who doesn't just philosophize about things, he goes out and does it, day in, day out. The things in this book are normal for him and countless other people I have filmed with over the years. My hope is that they will soon become normal for you (and me) as well.

DARREN WILSON
Director, *Finger of God* and *Furious Love*

One of the first things you'll notice about Chris Overstreet is that he is a man who has had a life-changing encounter with God the Father. From that encounter now flows a river of compassion and fire. His passion for others to experience that same life-transforming love is evident in all he does. *A Practical Guide to Evangelism—Supernaturally* isn't just a how-to book, it's a powerful "why" book as well. This book captures the core values of Heaven coming to the Earth. This is what it looks like when God Himself touches a leper or a broken heart. Applying what Chris writes about in this book will bring out the Lion in any lamb.

DANNY SILK
Sr. Management Team, Bethel Church, Redding, California
Author of *Culture of Honor* and *Loving Our Kids on Purpose*

I first met Chris eight years ago. He was helping me with some landscaping at my house, and at one point we needed to go to our local home improvement store to get some extra material. While shopping, Chris turned the place into a revival center—people were healed and prophesied to, so that they left encouraged and full of hope. I had never seen such risk, as he stepped out in words of knowledge for the customers and workers. Moreover, each person responded to the compassion that exuded from his countenance and communication.

I soon learned that Chris does not just oversee outreaches—he is an outreach! The principles and core values in this book are not just nice theories and theologies, but practical keys in representing God's goodness and kindness, which leads people to repentance. Chris has masterfully connected the core values of the Kingdom of God demonstrated throughout the Scripture, and the revival expression of Bethel Church with evangelism.

A Practical Guide to Evangelism—Supernaturally will equip, empower, and activate you into a lifestyle of supernatural ministry, resulting in more effective evangelism among your family, friends, and community. Reading and incorporating the principles and core values in this book will make you into a world changer!

KEVIN DEDMON
Pastoral Staff, Bethel Church, Redding, California
Author of *The Ultimate Treasure Hunt: A Guide to Supernatural Evangelism Tthrough Supernatural Encounters*

Contents

Foreword

Most all of us have been involved in some form of evangelism. It is the privilege and responsibility of every believer. The apostle Paul thought it was so important that he exhorted Timothy to *do the work of an evangelist*, even though that was not his primary gift. It is a ministry that everyone can do and the only one that must take place before time ends. The priority ministry of worship will continue throughout eternity, as will our ministry to the saints. But evangelism is only for now.

There is a great difference between being involved in evangelism and being an evangelist. For example, I have a burden for souls and have prayed accordingly. But Chris Overstreet weeps for them, constantly. I come alive when people come to Christ. But this author can't live without getting people "saved." I stand before a crowd and wait for the leading of the Lord on when to invite people to place their faith in Jesus. For Chris, the time is always *now*. The only question is *how*. Alhough Chris operates in great power, with miracles, signs, and wonders the norm, healing is never the goal. It is simply a tool to demonstrate the love of Jesus that it might draw people to Christ. For him every opportunity is the opportunity for people to be born again. Such is the life of a true evangelist.

In this day of increasing miracles, the salvation of a soul remains the single greatest miracle. In this season, evangelists are thriving not only in the stadiums of this world with the corresponding large crowds but wonderfully in the more simple public places, like the streets of our cities. This is where Chris mentors other evangelists so they'll always remember that each individual is important to God.

An evangelist is one part of the "fivefold ministry" (apostle, prophet, evangelist, pastor, and teacher) and thus is actually given to the church as a gift in order to hand out equipment to enable us to complete the Great Commission. Not often do we think of an evangelist as one who would have a ministry priority to the church. Because of the notion that the evangelist is to minister only to the lost, there is often a breakdown in the function of this gift. Their heart is supposed to be toward the world. But they cannot fulfill their purpose alone—they must equip everyone to take part in this great calling of winning the lost. Without them, it's way too easy to think that everything is actually about us. Evangelists remind us about "them." Chris is a true evangelist, equipping the church, and winning the lost.

A Practical Guide to Evangelism—Supernaturally is the target of this wonderful book by Chris Overstreet. It is a privilege to commend to you both the man and the message. Both are pure, powerful, without guile—and guaranteed to change your life. Chris lives what he writes. And by reading this book, you just might discover that the passion for souls is contagious.

BILL JOHNSON

Senior Pastor, Bethel Church, Redding, California

Author of *When Heaven Invades Earth* and

Face to Face with God

www.BJM.org

www.iBethel.org

Preface

Inside this book are keys that will help all believers experience supernatural evangelism as a lifestyle, not just an event. The goal behind this book is to help train and equip the Christian community to minister effectively to the world by demonstrating the Kingdom of God with love and power on a consistent basis. In this book, I have emphasized love as the foundation and motivation in touching the world.

With all this in mind, you will notice questions at the end of each chapter that can be used in group settings or individually. Often, it is good to think through and process what you just read, and these question will help facilitate this as well as provide an opportunity to put these principles into action.

My true desire and prayer is for every Christian who reads this book to be empowered and equipped to see Heaven's influence on earth multiplied by destroying the works of the devil.

Introduction

There is an unfolding natural desire in the world today for the supernatural. We can see it on TV and in books targeted to young adults and children. There is a call in the spirit like there was in Elijah's day as he faced the prophets of Baal for a showdown to determine who served the true God of power. As Elijah called down fire from Heaven, it was instantly revealed whose God was the true source of all power.

Today, many people are spiritually asleep. What we fail to realize is that we frequently enjoy entertaining church services with great sermons that promise change but deliver no power. Believers walk around like spiritual zombies, afraid to confront any sort of darkness we encounter as we live our lives. We have been deceived in thinking that God does not have the power to destroy the works of the devil. It has been easier for us to turn away and act as if nothing is wrong with the world. We bear the name of Christ, but have often denied the power that is within Christ, the anointed one, and the power that is within us as followers of Christ.

I believe that God is waking up the Church to be a people that will demonstrate His love and power to the world. The Kingdom message is in the air, and the Spirit of God wants to partner with ordinary people who will believe. *"For the earnest expectation of the creation eagerly waits for the revealing of the sons of God"* (Rom. 8:19). God wants to reveal to us that we are to partner with Him to receive the abundant life He paid for on the cross.

I became a Christian in 1996, and after fully committing my life to Christ in 1999, I immediately had a desire to share my faith with others. I was desperate to see the world around me changed. I began preaching on the streets and people began getting saved. I came to Redding, California, to attend Bethel School of Supernatural Ministry. As a student, I was really impacted by Kingdom core values. I learned a lot of things the hard way, and if I had known ten years ago what I know today, my ministry would have looked very different. The core values we minister from are just as vital as the ministry itself because they shape and influence the message we carry and the way that we deliver it.

The principles outlined in this book are tried and true methods of supernatural evangelism. As I grew in my walk with God and in my passion for evangelism, I began taking teams of students and people from the church to the street to do ministry. Our church has made it our goal to take the revival we've experienced within our services to the streets and into the community, believing that we are the catalysts to see Heaven come to Earth in our town. Our students have been activated, empowered, and guided into a lifestyle of the Supernatural from all denominational backgrounds. They regularly see signs, wonders, healings, and salvations on the streets of Redding, California.

I've shared these principles with other churches and seen phenomenal transformation, both in those doing the ministry and in those being ministered to. I believe that we've stumbled upon a key to winning nations to Christ. If we are willing to regularly submit ourselves to the leading of the Holy Spirit, and will choose to live a lifestyle of risk, we will be the supernatural answer that the world is waiting for.

The time is now! You have one life. How will you choose to live? What will you live for? If a story was to be written at the end of your life, what would it say and how would it inspire someone else to live?

Will your story bless people, but keep them calm and relaxed? If your life story doesn't challenge people to embrace opportunities to display the Kingdom of God with love and power, I question whether you are truly living life to your fullest, God-given potential.

This book will challenge you and has the potential to transform your outlook on ministry. I invite you to live life to its fullest by walking in your true inheritance as a son or daughter of God, a person who displays the Kingdom of God in all aspects of his or her life with victorious love and transforming power.

Chapter 1

KINGDOM MINDSET

Experiencing God's Love

God is good all the time, and His love establishes perfect identity in us. As we experience God's love, we are able to give that love away to the world.

> *To know the love of Christ which passes knowledge; that you may be filled with all the fullness of God. Now to Him who is able to do exceedingly abundantly above all that we ask or think, according to the power that works in us* (Ephesians 3:19-20).

To know God's love is to experience God's love. What we experience, we are able to give away to others. Mike Bickle, director of the International House of Prayer, Kansas City, says that lovers always get more work done than do workers!

God's love changes the world inside of us, which in turn changes the world around us. In 1996, I found myself at the bottom of a pit. While in a jail cell, I kneeled all 375 pounds of my weight onto my knees as I asked Jesus Christ to come into my heart and forgive me of all my sins. That day, I felt true love, and that love is what I get to give away to the world.

Many people try to muster up enough courage to share Christ with others, to prophesy, and to heal the sick. When we keep things simple, with our motivation being love, that love will open the door for other miraculous things to take place in and through our lives.

The King and His Kingdom

Jesus lived from another world. He was born of Heaven, and He worked to bring Heaven to earth.

In 1999, I heard Bill Johnson speak about the Kingdom of God while I was in Youth With A Mission (YWAM). He mentioned that Jesus brought His world with Him. My eyes were opened as he read certain scriptures of the Bible that day. When he finished reading, Bill asked the Holy Spirit to come and move amongst us. That day, our Discipleship Training School (DTS) class experienced another world invading our world. It was, and is, the Kingdom of God.

Our focus is Heaven, and our mandate is to bring it to earth.

Jesus' life displayed His kingly authority through demonstrations of miracles, signs, and wonders. Everything He did was dependent on the Spirit of God. If Jesus, as a man, needed the Spirit of God to demonstrate the Kingdom, then we need His Spirit as well!

Our Father in heaven, hallowed be Your name. Your kingdom come. Your will be done on earth as it is in heaven (Matthew 6:9-10).

Our focus is Heaven, and our mandate is to bring it to earth.

Living From Another Realm

Just as Jesus came to destroy the works of the devil, so are you sent to destroy the works of the devil. The works of the devil are the works that try to keep us from experiencing everything that Christ came to give us: abundant life on earth as it is in Heaven. Sin, sickness, and disease are from the devil and not from God. God is good, and the devil is bad. God is full of truth. The devil is a liar.

When our eyes are continually focused on Heaven, we live from a Heavenly perspective. God is good and in Heaven there is no sickness, sin, poverty, depression, anxiety, fear, pain, or rejection. What we see in Heaven is health, restoration, peace, redemption, divine relationship with Jesus, Heavenly encounters, hope, joy, and prosperity.

Colossians 3:2 says, *"Set your mind on things above, not on things on the earth."* To live from Heaven's reality is to have our minds developed into a Kingdom-culture mindset. The Holy Spirit is our helper, and He is committed to help us transform the way that we think, so that we line up with His Heavenly worldviews. We must be filled with the Holy Spirit and able to allow Him to work through us freely. The Holy Spirit empowers us to change our mind to a Kingdom mindset on an ongoing basis.

> *And do not be conformed to this world, but be transformed by the renewing of your mind, that you may prove what is that good and acceptable and perfect will of God* (Romans 12:2).

By having a transformed mind, we can know the will of God, which lets us demonstrate His will on earth. This lets us respond to people's needs without questioning God's intent.

Many of our teams position themselves to hear God's voice on a consistent basis as they go out into our community to minister to people. By having a transformed mind, their hearing becomes much clearer and they know that God wants to heal the whole person—spirit, soul, and body.

One of our teams prayed for a woman who was bedridden because of pain in her back. After prayer, the team members asked her to get up out of her bed and walk. She walked a little bit but still had discomfort. The next day, we saw her walking in our community. She was all dressed up and looked like a new woman because God touched her.

Becoming an Encounter

When we experience God, it changes the way we see the world and ourselves—what we see in us and around us. The same Spirit that raised Christ from the grave lives inside of us, and that Spirit longs to get out of us. The Holy Spirit enables us to become a walking encounter wherever we go.

> When the Day of Pentecost had fully come, they were all with one accord in one place. And suddenly there came a sound from heaven, as of a rushing mighty wind, and it filled the whole house where they were sitting. Then there appeared to them divided tongues, as of fire, and one sat upon each of them. And they were all filled with the Holy Spirit and began to speak with other tongues, as the Spirit gave them utterance.
>
> And there were dwelling in Jerusalem Jews, devout men, from every nation under heaven. And when this sound occurred, the multitude came together, and were confused, because everyone heard them speak in his own language. Then they were all amazed and marveled,

saying to one another, "Look, are not all these who speak Galileans? And how is it that we hear, each in our own language in which we were born? Parthians and Medes and Elamites, those dwelling in Mesopotamia, Judea and Cappadocia, Pontus and Asia, Phrygia and Pamphylia, Egypt and the parts of Libya adjoining Cyrene, visitors from Rome, both Jews and proselytes, Cretans and Arabs—we hear them speaking in our own tongues the wonderful works of God."

So they were all amazed and perplexed, saying to one another, "Whatever could this mean?"

Others mocking said, "They are full of new wine."

But Peter, standing up with the eleven, raised his voice and said to them, "Men of Judea and all who dwell in Jerusalem, let this be known to you, and heed my words. For these are not drunk, as you suppose, since it is only the third hour of the day. But this is what was spoken by the prophet Joel" (Acts 2:1-16).

When the believers were filled with the Spirit, they could not help but speak the word of God boldly. They had an encounter that changed their mindsets and allowed them to become an active encounter themselves.

The baptism of the Holy Spirit, which filled the believers, empowered them to be bold witnesses. The true baptism of the Holy Spirit is not just so that we can pray in tongues.

This is a wonderful gift, however, that is mentioned in First Corinthians chapter 12. The true baptism empowers us to be witnesses. Peter was empowered to overcome his past insecurities and fears. The one who denied Jesus three times was now the one filled with the Holy Spirit and fire, giving a mass call for the Jews to come to the knowledge of the Lord Jesus Christ.

Willingness to be an encounter for others changes the way we live. No longer do we live for ourselves. Instead, we live for others. It opens up our eyes to opportunities around us.

As we learn to live in God's presence, we realize who we really are. When we begin to see ourselves the way He sees us, our minds are changed to walk in the identity He has given us.

Questions to Ponder

1. How does God see me?

_____

_____

_____

2. How does God's love change the way that I see the world around me?

_____

_____

_____

3. How does knowing God's will empower me to demonstrate it on earth?

_____

_____

_____

4. How do my personal encounters with God allow me to become an encounter to others around me?

_____

_____

_____

Questions for Group Discussion

1. What are some signs of the true baptism of the Holy Spirit?

_____

_____

_____

2. How does being filled with the Holy Spirit empower us to be bold witnesses?

_____

_____

_____

3. Is there anyone in this group who has not been baptized in the Holy Spirit?

_____

_____

_____

Life Application

Ask the Holy Spirit to reveal to you any lies that you have believed about God and His Kingdom. Then ask the Holy Spirit to show you the truth.

Spiritual Exercise

Take time right now to get alone with God, and ask Him how He sees you. Wait on His presence. As you relax your mind, turn your heart's affection toward His presence and allow Him to speak to you. Ask Him to show you how He sees you through His love. While resting in God's presence, imagine the courage that lives inside of you is moving through your life to display great acts of God's power. If you can see it in your heart and you can believe it, it will become reality! You are a walking encounter.

Chapter 2

CORE VALUES OF EVANGELISM

What Is a Core Value?

Core values are the inner structure around which we build our lives. These are values or truths that influence our lives. Core values aren't just principles that we agree with. They are virtues that often motivate our decision-making as well as our actions.

Love

Love is active, not passive.

> *For God so loved the world that He gave His only begotten Son, that whoever believes in Him should not perish but have everlasting life* (John 3:16).

God is love and He is good. His love must be the foundation of everything we do in our lives. We love others with God's heart of love because He first loved us. It's the love of Christ that compels us to action, to find the gold and the potential in the lives of those around us. When we have the core value of love operating in us, we will evangelize—not because we have to, but because His love gives us the desire to.

I was in Africa years ago where we saw incredible miracles, signs, and wonders. Right before I was about to preach in a small crusade, the Lord spoke to me. He asked me this question: "Are you going to pray for the sick tonight just so you can see another miracle? Or are you going to pray for them because you love them?" Colossians 3:14 says, *"But above all these things put on love, which is the bond of perfection."*

> When we have the core value of love operating in us, we will evangelize—not because we have to, but because His love gives us the desire to.

Honor

Honor places a high worth on every person God has created, regardless of his or her social status or spiritual condition. Honor raises people up to the high calling that Jesus has for them. We honor people not for what we can get from them, but because we have been honored (raised up) by Jesus. We don't honor people for who they appear to be. We honor them for who Jesus says they are:

> *Having your conduct honorable among the Gentiles, that when they speak against you as evildoers, they may, by your good works which they observe, glorify God in the day of visitation* (1 Peter 2:12).

Years ago, I chased down a person in a power wheelchair because I wanted to see this man healed. After I asked him if I could pray for him, he resisted me. In the midst of him resisting me, I still tried to force him to receive prayer. What I didn't realize at the time is that I was not valuing or honoring him as a person. In that moment, he was nothing more than a project to me. The Lord taught me through this situation that regardless of someone's physical condition, he or she still deserves to be honored as a person.

Can you honor someone you don't agree with? There have been many situations where I've been placed in a conversation where I didn't agree with the other person's opinion. But because Jesus honors this person, I am still required to honor and love him or her. As believers, we should honor people regardless of whether we agree with them or not. It's not helpful to be disrespectful when presenting the Gospel to others. Our responsibility is to love and honor them all the time.

It is important that we see people as people, not as projects. John Maxwell says, "People don't care how much we know until they know how much we care."[1]

I was in a restaurant one time, and I disrupted the whole restaurant by standing up and preaching. The problem was not that I was preaching, but that I was not honoring the restaurant and the customers who were eating there. The owner of the restaurant was not impressed with my ability to preach, and he didn't ask me to come back. I should have used common sense and basic wisdom to understand that I was a disruption rather than a blessing.

Honoring people must come from a genuine heart of love regardless of what a person looks like, smells like, or even acts like. It also entails honoring your environment. You can still be bold, but at the same time you need to honor businesses and people around you. Use wisdom while ministering in business settings. One of your values should be to see businesses prosper.

Presence

And John bore witness, saying, "I saw the Spirit descending from heaven like a dove, and He remained upon Him. I did not know Him, but He who sent me to baptize with water said to me, 'Upon whom you see the

*Spirit descending, and remaining on Him, this is He who
baptizes with the Holy Spirit'"* (John 1:32-33).

Living in the presence of God is living with our heart's affection
turned toward Heaven. When the presence of God rests on ordinary
people, it changes the environment in which they live. We become
a host for God and for His Kingdom, which is what enables us to
demonstrate God's love and to manifest His Kingdom. Learning to
host the presence is a major key to walking in the supernatural.

Our teams will often ask people if they have ever felt or experienced the presence of God. On one occasion, a young man was asked
this in a park, and he said he had not. The team asked if he would
like to, and he said yes. He was instructed to hold his hands out.
As he did, a team member prayed that he would feel the person of
the Holy Spirit. As he began to feel the presence of God on him, he
described it as coolness or a tingling sensation running through his
body. After he experienced God's presence, he was asked if he would
like to receive Jesus into his heart. Without hesitation, he said yes!

Power

To live a life of miracles, signs, and wonders is not an option
but a Heavenly mandate. We need Heaven's assistance moving
through our lives to display the raw power of God. Miracles, signs,
and wonders point people to Jesus.

> *For our gospel did not come to you in word only, but also
> in power, and in the Holy Spirit and in much assurance,
> as you know what kind of men we were among you for your
> sake* (1 Thessalonians 1:5).

While picking up a friend of mine at the Sacramento Airport, I
walked by a group of women and told them that Jesus loved them.
To my surprise, ten minutes later one of the young women from

that group came over to me and asked if I could pray for her. I immediately said, "Yes, what can I pray for you about?" She said, "My lover just left me, and my children have been taken from me." She explained to me that she was living a lesbian lifestyle. I told her that Jesus loved her and Jesus had a plan for her life. I told her that Jesus could transform her. As I was speaking those very words into her heart, the atmosphere around us began to change. She was probably expecting me to tell her how bad of a sinner she was. But after I explained the love of the Father to her, her heart began to melt. I asked her, "Would you like to receive Jesus into your heart and to be forgiven of your sins?" She said yes! So I led her in a prayer to receive Jesus Christ into her heart and to ask Jesus to forgive her of her sins.

After praying with her, I asked her if it was okay for me to lay my hand on her head and pray for her while in the airport. She said yes. I said, "Are you ready?" She said yes. I said, "Are you sure?" And she said yes. As I asked her the last time, I felt the power of God come upon me. I felt faith arise in my heart and the power of God that was at hand to see this woman's life completely transformed. As I laid my hand upon her head and began to pray, she fell out cold in the airport under the power of God!

While she was lying on the ground, people started to surround her and ask if she was okay. They said they were available to call 911. I told them, "No, that's okay! She's having an encounter with God right now." Two or three other people came by and asked if she was okay and also offered to call 911. One of them was a police officer.

The last gentleman who came over to her asked me what was going on.? I told him she was having an encounter with God. He started to laugh in a mocking way. She sat up shortly after this gentleman began to mock her and said, "Let him laugh. He does not understand what just happened to me!" I said, "What did you feel when I laid my hand on your head?" She said, "I felt fire go through me." She explained to me that she was planning on going home and committing suicide that night. But because of the encounter she had just had with God, her life now had hope.

Jesus lived His life while being tapped into the power source of the Holy Spirit. He was on a mission to destroy the works of the devil. Power on display forces people to a decision.

> *And when He had called His twelve disciples to Him, He gave them power over unclean spirits, to cast them out, and to heal all kinds of sickness and all kinds of disease* (Matthew 10:1).

Jesus passed the baton of manifesting God's power and destroying the works of the devil to His disciples in the Great Commission. We are His disciples and these signs will follow those who believe.

Joy

The joy of the Lord empowers us to carry our own spiritual weather system. No matter the circumstances, the forecast over our lives is Heavenly rain and high glory winds that manifest through the joy of the Lord, *"...for the joy of the Lord is your strength"* (Neh. 8:10).

While I was buying a Gatorade at a gas station, a lady behind the counter looked at me and said, "What are you on?" I replied, "I've been doing a bit of drinking before I came here." She looked at me puzzled. I explained that I had been drinking a bit of the new wine. I was being filled with the Holy Spirit. I asked her, "Would you like some?" I waved my hand at her, and she bent over laughing uncontrollably! After paying for my Gatorade, I went on my way, and she was still laughing as I left the gas station.

Supernatural joy is very attractive to those who haven't experienced it. When joy is a core value, you can't help but leak the joy of the Lord onto others. When you are living in supernatural joy, you will radiate this joy and change the atmosphere around you. Unbelievers living with hopelessness and depression will be drawn to you, which make evangelism really easy.

Faith

Faith is spelled: R—I—S—K, with love and honor.

In 1999, I was hearing stories of people hearing God and responding to what God was saying. Some people told stories of how God would direct them to go to a certain location and they would meet a certain person whom God spoke to them about. In my heart, I said "WOW! How would that be—for God to use me that way." But could it really be possible? Could God use me like that? SO one day while in prayer, I was asking God, "Speak to me, Lord. I'll do anything You tell me to do." And I felt like the Lord told me to go to a certain location in the city that I was living in, and that I would find an individual on a certain street. I was so pumped up! It was my time to shine! So I gathered a couple of my friends and we headed out late that evening to follow the voice of God.

As we made our way to the city, I started to feel uneasy in my heart. We were not able to find the location that I thought the Lord had directed me to. And to top it off, there was no person I thought I would meet. We pulled over in the car and I started to get upset. I was upset at myself and I was thinking in my mind—"I knew it. This stuff is not for me. Supernatural evangelism is only for special and gifted people. After all, I have a past. Why would God want to use someone like me, after everything I had done in the past?" As I started to cry, my friends in the vehicle tried to cheer me up. One of my friends named Laura said to me, "Chris, you did not miss it tonight." And I responded, "What are you talking about? We couldn't find the place, and we couldn't find the person." She insisted, "Chris—you didn't miss it tonight." She went on to tell me that most people would do nothing with what they felt like the Lord showed them. Then she proceeded to tell me, "God is looking at your heart, Chris, and He loves your heart, because you have a heart of love and you are willing to take a risk for Him." That day I learned a valuable lesson. When my heart is motivated to love God and to follow His leading and to love people, I will never miss it. Like every child, it takes time to learn how to walk. A child takes a couple steps, then the child might fall down. But eventually, that child learns how to walk. Each of us who is born again is a child of God, and we all are learning how to walk this thing out with a Father who loves us and is proud of us when we take steps that require risk.

When you adopt a lifestyle of faith as a core value in your life, you will become aware of more Kingdom opportunities all around you.

Questions to Ponder

1. Why should love be our number one reason to demonstrate and share the Gospel of the Kingdom?

_____

_____

_____

_____

_____

2. Do I have these core values working in my life?

_____

_____

_____

_____

3. How can I honor people and businesses, or those in the workplace, while still having a passion to share Christ?

_____

_____

_____

_____

4. Why is the presence of God valuable in evangelism?

_____

_____

_____

_____

5. How does power on display bring people to a point of decision about Jesus?

_____

_____

_____

_____

6. Why is joy so attractive?

_____

_____

_____

_____

7. Why does faith require me to be active?

_____

_____

_____

_____

Questions for Group Discussion

1. What has been your motivation while evangelizing in the past?

_____

_____

_____

_____

2. Were there times in your past when you did not demonstrate these core values while ministering to others?

_____

_____

_____

_____

3. How do these core values transform the way that we think and act?

_____

_____

_____

_____

Life Application

Ask the Holy Spirit daily to develop these core values in your life until they are a part of you and look for opportunities (set goals starting today) to demonstrate them through your life.

Endnote

1. John Maxwell, *Relationships 101* (Nashville, Thomas Nelson, 2003).

Chapter 3

EVANGELISTS AND THOSE WHO EVANGELIZE

Fivefold Ministry

If you are not called to be an evangelist, can you evangelize? Jesus gave the Great Commission to more than the fivefold minister. In Mark 16, we see clearly that He gave this commission to every believer. Evangelism through demonstrations of love and power is not just for individuals behind the pulpit. It is for every individual who calls on the name of the Lord Jesus.

> And He said to them, "Go into all the world and preach the gospel to every creature."... And they went out and preached everywhere, the Lord working with them and confirming the word through the accompanying signs (Mark 16:15,20).

Many confuse the office of the evangelist with someone who evangelizes. The office of the evangelist is one of the fivefold gifts to the church mentioned in Ephesians 4:11-12.

Fivefold Ministers

And He Himself gave some to be apostles, some prophets, some evangelists, and some pastors and teachers, for the equipping of the saints for the work of ministry, for the edifying of the body of Christ (Ephesians 4:11-12).

In Kris Vallotton's prophetic book, *Basic Training for the Prophetic Ministry,*[1] he writes about the overview of the five governmental offices in the church. Included is a short description of their roles in the Body of Christ, which gives us a clear understanding and assistance in receiving their ministry into our lives.

The grace, or anointing, that is on the fivefold ministry is Christ's gift to the church for the equipping of the saints for the working of the ministry for the edifying of the Body of Christ.

> The grace, or anointing, that is on the fivefold ministry is Christ's gift to the church for the equipping of the saints for the working of the ministry for the edifying of the Body of Christ.

There is a different flavor of grace that rests on each position in the fivefold ministry. When you honor a fivefold minister, who is a gift to the Body of Christ, you draw on the Christ-given grace that is on his or her life.

Jesus is our main source of grace. But grace also flows through gifts that He has given to the church. These gifts are not to be confused with the gifts of the Holy Spirit that are listed in First Corinthians 12. The gifts listed in Ephesians chapter 4 are for people who are called to serve the Body of Christ and to give away what was freely given to them.

Jesus operated in all five offices of ministry while He was on earth. He had the same grace that each fivefold minister has. Just like you can receive this grace from a fivefold minister, you can receive directly from Jesus. But He puts people in our lives specifically to teach us about relationship and honor.

The Office of the Evangelist

The grace on an evangelist's life is to gather the lost and to bring them to Jesus. Fivefold evangelists live, eat, and breathe this passion. Their mind is constantly thinking about the lost and the condition of their hearts. The grace on an evangelist compels them to draw the lost into the presence of Jesus.

From a heart of compassion to see the world get saved, a true evangelist will often move in miracles, signs, wonders, as well as in deliverances. But that grace was never intended for him or her alone! Jesus gave it freely to them, so that they could give it away to the Body of Christ. Paul said that the fivefold minister is to equip the saints for the work of ministry (see Eph. 4). The grace that an evangelist imparts to the Body is typically a strong desire to see souls saved, healed, and delivered. They release boldness to proclaim and demonstrate the Kingdom of Heaven. Grace supernaturally empowers you to change the world around you.

A true evangelist will never condemn other believers by saying that they're not doing enough. A true evangelist, through the love of the Father, will impart grace to do more than enough. When believers receive grace from an evangelist, they will find evangelism to be easier than when they tried to do it with their own natural ability. Suddenly, they have the same supernatural desire and passion that an evangelist has. And they begin to supernaturally manifest the love of Jesus to the lost around them.

The Outflow of an Inward Commitment

Some are called to be an evangelist. But every believer is called to evangelize. It is one of the normal outflows of an inward commitment to Christ.

Often, we put people on pedestals and then think we can never be like that person. We may look at a prophet or an evangelist and think, "I could never do that." But we are called to do the same things Jesus did, and He operated in all five types of ministry. You are called to evangelize the world. And you can do that by ministering in your realm of influence.

If you are a teacher, you can model the character of Christ in the school system, and you can speak prophetic insight into the lives of your students. You grade papers all the time. You can write prophetic notes of encouragement that release supernatural grace on that student's life. If you are a businessman, your business is to bring Heaven to earth with an explosion of prosperity. If you are a doctor, you can use not only your natural ability gained through schooling and experience, but also the supernatural ability given by the Spirit who raised Christ Jesus from the grave and who lives in you. You can lay your hands on the sick and see them recover!

Every believer has a realm of influence to which they're called. Christ's love compels us to reach the world around us. Kevin Dedmon, author of *The Ultimate Treasure Hunt*, says, "We must have an encounter, so that we can become an encounter, so other people can have an encounter."[2] Every believer who has the Spirit of God inside him or her is a walking DA—divine appointment.

The Holy Spirit enables us, through our inner commitment to Christ, to reach the world around us. When the Holy Spirit is at work in and through our lives, people around us will encounter the love of Jesus in us, resulting in salvations, deliverances, miracles, signs, and wonders.

Two Examples of Modern Evangelists

Reinhard Bonnke

Reinhard Bonnke's life has been centered on faith. Bonnke started preaching the Gospel to crowds as small as five in South Africa. But through his faithfulness, those crowds began to multiply to hundreds, then thousands, then hundreds of thousands, and now millions. Faithfulness is a key to growing into the things God has for us.

Every believer possesses *"a measure of faith"* (Rom. 12:3). That measure of faith is like a muscle; the more we use the faith that the Lord has given us, the more we expand and grow in our influence.

You will see that measure of faith grow over time by being faithful, consistent, and hungry. Reinhard Bonnke didn't wake up one day and preach to millions. But as a little boy, the Lord told him that one day he would go to Africa and preach the Gospel there. As he grew up, he developed himself around the vision that God gave him to see Africa washed in the blood of the Lamb. His actions produced faith that grew in him over time. The faith that the Lord places in our lives, as we steward what has already been given to us, will grow until we accomplish our eternal purposes:

> *According to the eternal purpose which He accomplished in Christ Jesus our Lord, in whom we have boldness and access with confidence through faith in Him* (Ephesians 3:11-12).

Many people ask for more faith, but the question should be, "How should I use my faith?" Whatever faith or realm of influence God has given you will expand as you are faithful and diligent.

Carlos Anacondia

Carlos Anacondia from Argentina moves in an incredible deliverance ministry. In the 1980s, when Carlos Anacondia held crusades in Argentina, people would demonically manifest miles away from the event as the power of God was released. His teams would bring people to a big deliverance tent and see their spirits, souls, and bodies get radically delivered.

Ordinary believers can move in deliverance as well. It's not just for someone who stands behind a pulpit in a large arena, or for the leader of a deliverance ministry in a church. There are people in your communities who won't come to a big meeting, but they're in desperate need of deliverance. They're under the powerful influence of the enemy, and they want freedom. Our job is to represent Jesus in the marketplace, the workplace, and in the communities that we live in. Jesus has empowered us to change our communities instead of simply living in them.

The Saints

The saints are Christ's body on earth, commissioned to plunder hell and to populate Heaven.

Reinhard Bonnke often says that he believes that there will be more people in Heaven than there are in hell because hell was not created for people. Hell was created for the devil and his demons.

When the saints arise with fire in their eyes, with the realization that they are Christ's voice, hands, and feet of love to the world, nothing will hold us back. One of the most exciting things we get to do is to introduce people to a life-transforming relationship with Jesus.

> *God was in Christ reconciling the world to Himself, not imputing their trespasses to them, and has committed to us the word of reconciliation. Now then, we are ambassadors for Christ, as though God were pleading through us: we implore you on Christ's behalf, be reconciled to God. For He made Him who knew no sin to be sin for us,*

that we might become the righteousness of God in Him
(2 Corinthians 5:19-21)

God calls us "ambassadors of reconciliation" and wants to make His appeal to people through us!

An ambassador is someone who officially represents one country to another. As believers, we get to represent Heaven to earth and to bring Heaven's world to this world. Ambassadors are given authority from their home nation to influence the nation that they visit. As ambassadors of Christ, we have been given both power and authority to represent Christ supernaturally in the world that we live in.

An ambassador does not just have one kind of personality. If you are assuming you have to be loud, outgoing, and fearless to make a difference in the world around you, you have bought into a religious lie. You don't need to look, talk, or act like someone else to evangelize. God has created your unique personality to reach those people in your realm of influence. You'll be most effective when you relax and be yourself and allow the grace of God to flow through you as you interact with the people around you.

Questions to Ponder

1. How does the Great Commission involve evangelism?

_____

_____

_____

2. What is the purpose of the fivefold gifts mentioned in Ephesians 4:11?

_____

_____

_____

3. How do the grace or strengths of an evangelist differ from other fivefold gifts?

_____

_____

_____

Questions for Group Discussion

1. In your daily life, what are some ways you can influence people around you?

_____

_____

_____

_____

2. What does it mean to be an ambassador of reconciliation?

_____

_____

_____

_____

_____

Life Application

Learn to recognize the grace and giftings on those that are around you, as well as recognize those who Christ has put in your life. We are rewarded for honoring those in the fivefold ministry by receiving the supernatural grace that they can impart to us.

Endnotes

1. Kris Vallotton, *Basic Training for the Prophetic Ministry* (Shippensburg, PA: Destiny Image Publishers, 2005).

2. Kevin Dedmon, *The Ultimate Treasure Hunt: The Ultimate Guide to Supernatural Evangelism Through Supernatural Encounters* (Shippensburg, PA: Destiny Image Publishers, 2007).

Chapter 4

OVERCOMING REJECTION AND FEAR

The Battlefield of Fear and Faith

Years ago, I wanted to share my faith, but I was afraid. I decided to wear a Christian T-shirt to Wal-Mart, which, at first, was very hard for me to do. I knew that people might ask me about the message on my shirt, so I felt like I had to be ready to share the Gospel. Although I started at that simple level, I grew in faith as I continued pushing past my fear and growing in God.

Many times when we see someone with great boldness or power, we often assume that person has always been that way. This is not the case for a lot of people, and it definitely wasn't this way for Peter.

Peter was a man just like us. Often his fear and insecurities got the best of him. One time, his fear almost motivated him to murder someone, an incident that resulted in him cutting off a soldier's ear with a sword (see John 18:10).

Even though Peter denied Jesus three times, Jesus' love and grace empowered Peter to step into his God-given destiny to be a spiritual rock (see Luke 22:54-62; Matt. 16:18). You may feel afraid, or you might compare yourself to someone else and come up short, but it's important to know that God's love and grace will strengthen you just like it did Peter. It is God who brought Peter into his destiny, and as you trust the Lord, He will bring you into yours.

Fear is paralyzing and feels like a wall at times. One of the greatest struggles that believers deal with is fear—the fear of the unknown, fear of rejection, or fear of confrontation. If I was the devil (which I'm not!), one of the things I would do is put fear into believers and try to keep them from speaking because they have the power of life in their tongues.

Fear says, "You can't do it." Under the influence of fear, you feel small, insignificant, and trapped. Under the influence of faith, all things are possible. You see the end result. You are looking from Heaven's perspective. These two forces—Heaven and hell—are at war with each other. The great news is that Jesus, our victorious warrior, has overcome the enemy. When we partner with Jesus, our fight against fear has already been overcome.

Dreaming With God

A testimony is waiting for you on the other side of fear because you've faced a great test. We get beyond the wall of fear by dreaming with God using our sanctified imagination. We must see ourselves doing great miraculous works. If we can first see it in our hearts, it will become reality.

God has given us our imagination, and when we give it back to Him (when it is "sanctified"), He empowers us to dream with Him.

Years ago, I would go into my bedroom and imagine myself praying for the sick and seeing them recover. Often I would get down on my knees and imagine that I was out on the street praying for someone who had a problem with his knee. I asked the imaginary man if I could lay my hands on his knee and pray for his healing. It was all happening in my imagination. I would interview him after praying and ask him, "How does it feel now?" And he'd say, "All the pain is gone!" I would get so excited and I'd say, "All the pain's gone! Praise God!"

I would also imagine myself leading people to the Lord. I would imagine the encounters and the conversations. My imagination empowered me to look for opportunities for my dreams to become reality.

As we see these dreams come alive in us, we can take them to God and ask for these opportunities. We should seek opportunities that put a demand on the faith that lives inside of us. If you can see the dream and believe in the dream, the dream can become reality.

Keys to Overcoming Fear:

▶ Dream with God.

▶ Review testimonies and make them personal to you.

▶ Hang around with people who are bolder than yourself.

▶ Ask God for opportunities in your daily life to grow and step out.

▶ Take risks. Faith in action (through love and honor) is spelled R-I-S-K.

▶ Keep a prayer journal to record the dreams in your heart and what the Lord is speaking to you.

▶ Be in environments where faith is put into action (faith-filled conferences, mission trips, home groups, etc.).

▶ Set spiritual goals of what you are going to step out and accomplish.

▶ Feed the fire and passion in your heart by listening to CDs, reading books, studying biographies of great revivalists, watching DVDs, listening to classic sermons, and feeding on things that inspire you to take risks for God.

▸ What you focus on is what you become—don't focus on your shortcomings; instead focus on the greatness that's inside you and who God is saying you are going to be.

▸ Change your self-talk—look yourself in the mirror every day and tell yourself who God says you are. Remind yourself of what He has done for you, what He is doing, and what He wants to do in and through you

▸ Just go out there and do it; it is okay to be nervous as you go.

Love Has No Fear

God's love establishes perfect identity. When we know who we are, we're not afraid to step out and do the things God says we can do.

> *You are a chosen generation, a royal priesthood, a holy nation, His own special people, that you may proclaim the praises of Him who called you out of darkness into His marvelous light* (1 Peter 2:9).

Being chosen is empowering. It empowers us because we know we are loved. This means we are no longer stepping out *for* the favor of God. Now, we can step out *from* the favor of God. When we know this, we know that God is with us and His hands are upon us. This changes our expectations for what God can do through us because He has chosen to use us. He wants us to proclaim the praises of Him who called us out of darkness into His marvelous light.

What we meditate on is what we become. God commanded Joshua to be strong and very courageous (see Josh. 1:6). Then God gave him insight on how to be strong and very courageous:

> *This Book of the law shall not depart from your mouth,*
> *but you shall meditate in it day and night, that you*
> *may observe to do according to all that is written in it...*
> (Joshua 1:8).

Joshua set himself up for success by speaking God's Word and meditating on it day and night. The definition for meditate is to muse over, ponder, to plan in the mind, to purpose or intend. The Greek word means to revolve something in the mind, and is also translated to imagine.

Meditating and declaring God's promises are vital for you to become everything you have been created to be. Our words have power behind them. We can either bring life or death through our spoken words. In my life, I have found that declaring God's Word over my life empowers me to walk in the love that overcomes fear.

Redemptive, Proactive Mindsets

Repeat these Kingdom truths over yourself every day until they become a normal part of your thinking. Soon, your actions will change because you are thinking God's thoughts about yourself.

- ▶ I choose to love because I am loved.

- ▶ My identity is anchored in Christ and secure in His love.

- ▶ I am as bold as a lion.

- ▶ I am not afraid of being around people who are greater than me.

- I am always looking for the gold God has placed in me.

- I tell myself what I can do, and then I do it.

- I look for creative ways to impact the world around me.

- I look for ways to serve others around me, so I can see them step into their greatness.

- I believe that the great "I Am" who lives inside me produces greater works through me (John 14:12).

- I don't have to work for love; I work from love.

- I know that when I walk into a room, I change the atmosphere because of the Holy Spirit who lives in me.

- I have the unlimited resources of Heaven to give away to anyone, in any place, at any time.

- I will not compare myself with others because I am unique and significant.

- I will not be jealous of others who are greater than myself, but I will rejoice with them in their accomplishments.

- I am a walking encounter.

- I have the favor of God on my life.

- I am who He says I am, and I will do what He says I can do.

- Miracles, signs, and wonders are a normal part of my life, and they follow me as I follow Christ.

- I live a life of faith and today is going to be the best day of my life so far.

Faith Is Spelled R-I-S-K

If you are not willing to take a risk, you will never be able to move in the supernatural. Fear of the unknown causes many people to live inside a box. This box of fear may feel safe and protecting, but it is really a prison.

> It can be very inconvenient, but if we're willing to trust God and take a risk as we step out in faith, we will see great miracles take place.

Most of the miracles, signs, and wonders that our teams see in the community require them to take a risk. It can be very inconvenient, but if we're willing to trust God and take a risk as we step out in faith, we will see great miracles take place. James 2:26 says, *"For as the body without the spirit is dead, so faith without works is dead also."*

While stepping out in faith by taking risks, it is important that we remember to be motivated by love. The people we are ministering to need to feel loved and honored. They're people, not projects. God wants us to step out in faith so that we release miracles to people around us, but we need to be careful that our risks don't become dishonoring.

Dealing With Rejection

Most of us have experienced rejection in the past. In many of us, this has bred fear and insecurity, which eventually becomes a prison. We must destroy the walls of this prison of rejection so that we can be free to manifest the Kingdom of God.

If you are rejected (or feel rejected), remember that your source of love and security (the opposite of insecurity) comes from God, not man. Instead of wallowing in a feeling of rejection, turn it around by looking for people you can love. When you love people, it enables your focus to turn away from yourself toward other people. You can supernaturally draw from Heaven to overcome rejection by rooting yourself in His love and getting out of yourself. You will be so filled with the love of Jesus that you will forget your old identity as "the rejected one" and live your identity as "the accepted and loved one." As Mike Bickle says, lovers get more done than workers.

Many people get discouraged if someone rejects them the first time that they are stepping out. They may take that rejection personally, and it can create a momentum of fear in their lives that says, "I'm never going to do this again."

It's important to realize that people aren't rejecting you! They're rejecting what you have to say—what you are offering them. When our heart is motivated by love, we will look past rejection.

Even as we step out, we may still experience the feeling of rejection. Most people have experienced rejection at some point and, because it was so painful, they developed a fear of rejection. If we experience rejection when we step out in faith, we need to go to God and ask Him to take away the pain of rejection, and ask Him to help us not take it personally. Then we can ask Him to fill in the hole, which was left by the pain, with His powerful love. Learning to do this will quickly get you connected to God's love in an authentic way that will give you strength and boldness. The pain and fear of rejection should have no place in a believer's life. God's love casts out all fear. Let's get connected to His heart so we can live out our destiny!

Questions to Ponder

1. What does the battle against fear look like for you?

   _____

   _____

   _____

2. How are you learning to overcome fear?

   _____

   _____

   _____

3. Why does it require faith to take risk?

   _____

   _____

   _____

4. How does declaring God's promises in the Word over your life empower you to think and act differently?

   _____

   _____

   _____

5. How does dreaming with God give you a hunger to walk in a supernatural lifestyle?

   _____

   _____

   _____

Questions for Group Discussion

1. Give an example of a time when fear prevented you from stepping out. If that same opportunity were presented to you again, what would you do differently?

    _____

    _____

    _____

2. Talk about a time in your life when you stepped past your fear by doing something for God. What were the results and what did you realize about the fear that tried to hold you back?

    _____

    _____

    _____

    _____

Chapter 5

THE PURPOSE OF SUPERNATURAL EVANGELISM

A Loving Father Always Gives of Himself

A father who tells his kids that he loves them, but never backs those precious words with action that display his love, proves that he is just giving lip service.

God said that He loves the world and desires that all men should be saved and come into the knowledge of the truth (see 1 Tim. 2:4). Those are not just words that sound nice, but they are backed up with action. God sent His only Son, Jesus Christ, to die in our place:

> *For God so loved the world that He gave His only begotten Son, that whoever believes in Him should not perish but have everlasting life. For God did not send His Son into the world to condemn the world, but that the world through Him might be saved* (John 3:16-17).

Love is always full of action. When we say that we love Jesus, those are action-filled words. When we say that we love our neighbor, those should be action-filled words as well. Jesus lives inside of us, so that we can love the world around us. Just as God sent His Son into the world (His love in action), He is sending us into the world as well. Just as Jesus was dependent on the Holy Spirit, we have the opportunity to be dependent on the Holy Spirit as well. Jesus handed us the baton and He says, "Now you go and do likewise!" (See Luke 10:37.)

Compassion Is the Key to Unlock the Hearts of Humanity

The word *compassion* does not mean merely to have pity on someone who is less fortunate. Instead, it is full of passion fueled with God's love to motivate us to action. Jesus demonstrated true compassion throughout His ministry. Matthew 14:14 says, *"And when Jesus went out He saw a great multitude; and He was moved with compassion for them, and healed their sick."*

Jesus never healed anyone out of selfish motives, nor to build His own ministry. Nor did He heal, then feed the five thousand, to bring a sense of self-worth. All the signs and the wonders that Jesus performed—and is still performing today—are through this very compassionate thing called love. Jesus befriended sinners when the ones who proclaimed to know God shunned them. And to make things worse, these *righteous ones* were afraid of them. They thought if they were around sinners, they would become spiritually contaminated.

What was the key that opened the hearts of these sinners? It was the key of compassionate love demonstrated through great acts of power, not just talk.

The Purpose of Supernatural Evangelism

In the summer of 2002, I had a chance to go to Africa to preach. I was having a great time. We saw many miracles take place. We saw the blind see, the deaf hear, and even the lame walk!

While I was getting ready to preach the Gospel in an open-air meeting, the Lord spoke to me. As clear as can be, He said, "Are you going to pray for the sick tonight just to see another miracle? Or are you going to pray for them tonight because you love them?"

I realized at that moment that my motivation was just to have another story that I could tell my friends back in the States. I was convicted for my lack of love and repented of my selfish attitude. After I repented, I continued to pray for the sick along with the team who accompanied me. We saw great breakthroughs demonstrated by God's love in power.

The purpose of supernatural evangelism is to display a God of love and power to a world that is in need of a Savior. Miracles, signs, and wonders manifested through individuals like you and me point other individuals to the Creator of the universe. Signs and wonders are directions to the King and His Kingdom. Power on display causes people to make choices. Wherever Jesus went, He displayed power while being dependent on the Holy Spirit. The power that He displayed caused many people to decide whether to follow Him or not.

Many of those who opposed and didn't follow Him were religious leaders of the day; so it still is today.

Ordinary People Displaying an Extraordinary God

The Holy Spirit is Christ's gift to us as believers, enabling us to live as Christ lived on the earth. Christ knew that we would need help and that it would be impossible to live a supernatural lifestyle apart from His Spirit. If Jesus needed the Holy Spirit while on the Earth, how much more do we?

However, if Jesus did all the miracles that He did by just being God, then we would have hundreds of reasons why we can't do what He did. But since He lived as a man completely dependent on the Spirit of God, we have no excuse why we can't do what He did!

Most assuredly, I say to you, he who believes in Me, the works that I do he will do also; and greater works than these he will do, because I go to My Father (John 14:12).

The Holy Spirit is changing the world inside of us to change the world around us. The same Spirit who raised Christ from the grave lives in each believer. That is the resurrection power living within us. The Holy Spirit does not just want to live in us, but wants to partner with us through right relationship to point other people into a radical saving relationship with Jesus Christ.

> The Holy Spirit does not just want to live in us, but wants to partner with us through right relationship to point other people into a radical saving relationship with Jesus Christ.

The Holy Spirit has never gone on vacation. He is still active in the earth today and is daily drafting individuals to openly display the raw power of God to all humanity.

Shouldn't I Wait Until My Character Is Developed?

Sometimes Jesus picks the most unlikely individuals who the world would never think would be great. Look at Peter as an example. Did he have it all together?

Jesus called Peter to follow Him while he was still a fisherman. As he followed Jesus, Peter saw all kinds of miracles take place right in front of him. Then, as a part of his internship, Jesus sent him to go do the same with the other disciples: to preach the Kingdom of God and to display it publicly:

And when He had called His twelve disciples to Him, He gave them power over unclean spirits, to cast them out, and to heal all kinds of sickness and all kinds of disease (Matthew 10:1).

Peter was a new follower of Jesus. But Jesus believed in him despite the areas in Peter's life that should have disqualified him. Peter was qualified because of his love for Jesus and his faith in Jesus.

What qualifies us is our love and faith. If we keep the Gospel simple and keep the love of God at the forefront of everything that we do and say, then the Holy Spirit who lives inside of us will transform us daily to be the individual we are called to be. Don't wait ten years to allow your character to be developed before you evangelize. Focus on what God has done in your life, and what He is doing in your life, and what He is going to do in and through your life. *"Arise, shine; for your light has come!"* (Isa. 60:1a).

Questions to Ponder

1. Why should love be the motivation for everything we do?

   _____

   _____

   _____

2. What is the purpose of supernatural evangelism, and how does that fit into your daily life?

   _____

   _____

   _____

3. How is God's love full of action?

   _____

   _____

   _____

4. How can ordinary people display an extraordinary God?

   _____

   _____

   _____

5. Are you waiting for your character to be developed before stepping out and doing extraordinary things?

   _____

   _____

   _____

Questions for Group Discussion

1. How do you respond when you feel compassion for people?

_____

_____

_____

2. How is supernatural evangelism different in a team than when you are on your own?

_____

_____

_____

Life Application

As you are in your daily prayer time this week, seek God's heart of compassion that can unlock people's hearts. Then look for opportunities that require God's heart of compassion to be manifested in extraordinary ways.

Chapter 6

PRAYING FOR THE SICK IN PUBLIC

These Signs Will Follow Those Who Believe

Have you ever heard a testimony of someone being healed in public and then thought to yourself, "How did they approach them and pray, let alone see them be healed?"

In this chapter, you will discover keys that will help you be more effective in ministering God's love and power in public to those who need healing.

For about six months, I carried a flash card in my pocket with this verse:

And these signs will follow those who believe: In My name they will cast out demons; they will speak with new tongues; they will take up serpents; and if they drink anything deadly, it will by no means hurt them; they will lay hands on the sick, and they will recover (Mark 16:17-18).

I would read this passage and then tell myself, "I am a believer and I will lay my hands on the sick and they will recover." Sometimes

I would say this to myself 50 times a day. The good news about this verse is that it is for every believer, saint, and person who serves an extraordinary God.

Many times, people feel like they are condemned to be spectators in the audience (sitting in the pews at church), only watching the game (supernatural ministry), but never being allowed to participate.

The church was never intended to just be in a building. It was supposed to be mobile and active with God's love and power.

How I Learned the Hard Way

Years ago, I made a lot of messes that could have been avoided. I lacked understanding on how to approach someone in a way that makes him or her feel honored and valued. I want to help you avoid the mistakes I've made by giving you some practical keys to pray for the sick in public. But these keys are not formulas. They are just a way for you to get started. As you are starting out, learn to rely on the Holy Spirit, who will be your guide.

How you approach people will vary from person to person. You are going to approach a person differently depending on the person's age, their gender, or the circumstances. Every individual should be approached with love and honor.

The Approach

Jesus never healed the sick the same way twice. Through His relationship with the Holy Spirit, Jesus was aware of the way the Father wanted to heal people. With that being said, there are many ways God will use you to see other people healed. To begin with, I recommend getting comfortable with approaching people with the following prayer model. Remember, this is not a formula but a key that will help you open a door to make this a normal part of your life, not just an outreach experience.

How you approach people will vary from person to person. You are going to approach a person differently depending on the person's age, their gender, or the circumstances. Every individual should be approached with love and honor.

Imagine that you've just finished dinner with two friends at a restaurant. As you are leaving, you see a man limping with his wife by his side. Your heart is moved with compassion for this man as you notice that he walks with a cane because of pain in his body.

When approaching someone, remember that love is the key to hearts. I would usually approach the person in this manner:

1. Walk up to the person and say something like, "Excuse me, sir. I noticed you appear to be in pain. Do you mind if I ask you what happened?" Say this in a calm, confident voice. Let the person explain.

2. Ask, "Is it all right if I pray for you right now?"

   a. Often, people will say yes, thinking that you intend to pray for them later when you are by yourself. Feel free to explain to them that you would like to pray for them now and ask if you can lay your hand on them to release God's power.

3. If the person wants prayer, ask if it is okay to place your hand on his or her body (if it is an appropriate place). If it is not appropriate, you can offer to place your hand on his or her shoulder or the person you are praying for could put his or her hand on the area of their body that has pain.

4. If the person just wants to talk about how bad their ailment is, gently guide the conversation back to

God's love by saying, "God loves you and wants to heal you. Let's pray right now."

5. Pray.

    a. Remember, this is not the time to pray, "God, if it is Your will...." Heaven is our model. God's will is already established in Heaven, and we are to pray from Heaven to Earth. There is no pain, sickness, or disease in Heaven. Your job is to declare that Heavenly reality by commanding all pain, sickness, or disease in the person's body to leave.

    b. Be at peace when you start to pray.

    c. Don't shout in tongues if you pray in tongues. In fact, don't shout at all. It's not necessary.

    d. Keep your eyes open when you pray because you will want to see the miracle.

    e. Don't pray long. Keep it to 30 seconds. Jesus did not pray long prayers to get people healed. It is not your prayer that heals them; it's your faith in action.

    f. Simply command all the pain to leave the person's body in Jesus' name.

6. Ask them, "What are you feeling? What's happening in your body? Can you try doing something that you couldn't do before without pain?"

    a. Ask people to try to do something they could not do before. For example, if they had knee problems, ask them to try something like knee bends or walking up stairs to see what God has done. Many times, we see people get healed while they are testing it out because they are stepping out in faith.

b. If people can't test it out, ask them if they felt change in their body after you prayed.

c. When someone is experiencing a healing or miracle in their body, sometimes the person may feel heat, tingling, coolness, peace, or joy. Other times they may not feel anything at all.

d. Ask people, "If the pain was at a ten, and we are praying for it to be zero, what number is the pain now?" This will give you a good sense of what has happened other than "It's better." Now, you'll know how much better.

e. If people tell you they are now at a five or six (in other words, they're getting better but not totally healed yet) ask them if you can pray again. Thank the Lord for the healing that is occurring and then command all remaining pain to go.

f. Remember that even Jesus had to pray for a blind man twice (See Mark 8:22-26). If He had to pray more than once for the man to be healed, we shouldn't be afraid to keep pushing forward in faith until the healing is complete.

7. When people are healed, point them to Jesus. Explain to them that it was Jesus who just healed them. Remember, signs and wonders are always intended to point people to Jesus. If they don't know Jesus, explain the Gospel to them. See Chapter 8 to learn about how to lead someone into a relationship with Jesus.

8. Let them know that, as believers, they will have access to the same power and authority over pain, sickness, and disease that you have just displayed. They can look forward to a love relationship with Jesus and a lifestyle of power.

9. If the person is with their family or friends, ask if any of them need to be healed of anything.

   a. Jesus said, *"Freely you have received, freely give"* (Matt. 10:8). The person who was just healed can turn around and release the healing into their friend or family member.

   b. If someone in the group says yes, use this as a coaching opportunity for the person who was just healed. Walk them through what you just did to teach them to do the same thing. Remind the person that as a believer, these signs will follow. Supernatural healing is a normal part of the Kingdom of God and is available to every believer.

   c. As the person is releasing healing to their friend or family, coach them along the way. Teach them to rejoice for what God is doing in them and through them. Celebrate their victory!

Ways People Are Healed in Public

By the Presence of God

We often hear testimonies of people being healed when no one lays hands on them, where the person is actually healed by the presence of God. When you feel comfortable, I encourage you to ask Jesus to lay His hands on the area where the person needs healing. Pray with Jesus without laying your hands on them and see what happens. Faith in action requires risk.

The Word of Knowledge

Sometimes you may receive a word of knowledge for healing. When this happens, faith is released in the atmosphere for healing. For more information on healing words of knowledge, see Chapter 9.

The Joy Treatment

Often when Jesus manifests His joy in the atmosphere, people are healed. The joy of the Lord is their strength.

Songs of Deliverance

We have heard many testimonies of people being healed in public after someone led by the Spirit has sung over them.

Healing Art

As they're led by the Spirit, people have drawn small pictures and have given them away to people. The presence of the Lord on the art has healed the person.

The Authority of the Spoken Word

Psalm 107:20 says, *"He sent His word and healed them, and delivered them from their destructions."* We have heard reports from some team members who have felt great authority arising in their heart. As they have commanded pain, sickness, or disease to leave someone's body, healing was released through the authority of the spoken word.

The Hug of Compassion

I love hearing stories about people who have received healing after someone has given them a hug of love. Sounds like something Jesus would do.

The Shadow of a Person

It is possible to be filled with God's presence so much that even your shadow can heal someone (see Acts 5:14-16).

Through Forgiveness

Many times we have seen people healed after they have forgiven someone who has hurt them

What If They Are Not Healed?

If the person is not being healed, never condemn them by saying they don't have enough faith, or that they are not holy enough to be healed. It's important that every person you pray for feels love coming from you. Jesus never condemned anyone who wanted to be healed.

Explain the difference between a healing and a miracle to the person. A miracle usually happens very fast while a healing, at times, can be a progressive work. In Acts chapters 3 and 4, a man who was paralyzed for years received prayer and was instantly made whole. This was a miracle.

Sometimes, healing can be a progressive work of God. It's important to explain to them that as you are praying, something is taking place. It's impossible to pray and have nothing happen.

Have them keep testing their body throughout the day. Often as they are walking away and thanking the Lord for His love and power, they will suddenly notice a change while testing and looking for their healing. Sometimes I will ask the person, "Do you have any unforgiveness in your life? Is there someone in your life who may have hurt you and you haven't released them of it?" Unforgiveness often hinders people from receiving their healing. This could be why they cannot be healed at this moment.

If they say, "I don't know," ask them if you can pray for the Holy Spirit to reveal to them if they do or not.

I'll pray by saying, "Holy Spirit, show them if they have any unforgiveness." Then I'll ask them, "With your eyes closed, does anyone come to your mind?"

If they say no, I say, "Okay." Then I will say, "God bless you. I'll be praying for you but know that Jesus loves you and He's doing something in your body even though you may not sense it."

If someone does come to their mind, I will lead them through a deliverance prayer similar to this. I'll say, "Repeat after me: Jesus, I forgive (the person's name) for everything they've done to me and everything they haven't done for me. I release you right now in Jesus' name. I break the power of unforgiveness."

Then I'll pray, "Holy Spirit, is there anyone else this person needs to forgive?" If so, I'll go through the same process until there is no one else they need to forgive.

I end the prayer session in a similar way by having them pray this: "Jesus, thank You for forgiving me and empowering me to forgive other people. I release them all to you and I break the power and the chains of unforgiveness. Holy Spirit, come and fill me with your peace and Your presence. I receive my healing right now in Jesus' name." Once again, have them try to do something they couldn't do before to see what God just did in their body.

How Should We Respond If They Don't Want Prayer?

When I approach people, the first thing I want to do is to build rapport with them. If I see that they are comfortable with me but not comfortable with prayer, I'll keep chatting with them and build more rapport. My first job is to love them and honor them. Building rapport shows that I care about them and I don't see them as just a project.

At some point, I'll ask them again if I can pray for them to be healed. If they say yes, I'll pray for them. If they say no, I'll say, "God bless you and have a great day." I won't force myself on them because my job is to love and serve them in whatever way they allow. In this case, my job is done.

It's important that they have a good experience with you because there will be other Christians who will come to them in the future. Often, our job is to sow a seed in someone's heart. When they feel loved and honored by Christians, this helps create an opportunity for the next person who comes along and wants to pray for them.

Ministering in a Business Setting

One of our goals as Christians should be to see businesses prosper. If we are loud and rude to people around us when we are in a business such as a restaurant or at a department store, we automatically lose our favor and the ability to influence people around us.

We also potentially discourage customers in that business. Walking in love and honor not only benefits the people we are approaching, but it also profits the business setting we are in. A business's primary job is to serve customers and make a profit, which is a Kingdom goal. If we forget this, we will dishonor the business owners by preventing them from accomplishing that Kingdom goal. If that happens, we may be asked to leave and not return. That means we have lost an area of influence in our community.

Walking in power demands wisdom. If you have a team of people with you, don't overwhelm customers by surrounding them with your whole team. Remember that they are there to shop. Have no more than two to three people approach an individual that you want to minister to. Have one of those people lead the conversation while the other two back them up.

Leadership is important even in a team of only two or three because insecurities in team members can cause problems. If there isn't a team leader, everyone may try to steer the ship and it may not get anywhere.

If someone on your team gets a word of knowledge for a specific person, have him or her grab somebody else on the team and approach the person. The team leader can say something like, "Excuse me. Hi, my name is Chris. I know you are busy shopping but I had a sense that the Lord wanted to heal you. By any chance, do you have any pain in your right shoulder?" If they're open to prayer, then go for it. If not, honor the reason that they are there, which is to shop. Send them on their way with a blessing.

Even though you are out doing ministry, it's okay to shop at the stores you are in. Supernatural evangelism should be a normal part of our day rather than an event. For more about evangelism as a normal part of our lifestyle, see Chapter 7 on, "Becoming a Super-natural Shopper."

Questions to Ponder

1. How does healing the sick fall in line with the Great Commission?

_____

_____

_____

2. As a believer, have you expected the Lord to use you in miracles, signs, and wonders prior to reading this book? Do you expect Him to do so now?

_____

_____

_____

3. How does it make someone feel if you force yourself on him or her when they don't want healing?

_____

_____

_____

4. What should our response be if a person does not want prayer?

_____

_____

_____

5. If a person isn't getting healed when you are praying for them, is it okay to blame them for not having enough faith?

_____

Questions for Group Discussion

Ask someone in your group to imagine they have a hurt body part. Do a walk through of the prayer model in this chapter. Introduce yourself, ask the person what the problem is, and ask if it would be okay to lay your hand on that part of their body if it's appropriate. Do an imaginary sanctified activation. This is to help your group have confidence and faith to do it out in public.

Life Application

Look for people in your community you can approach who need physical healing. You can either do this on your own or with another person. When you find someone, use the methods of approach mentioned in this chapter and bring a heart of love and honor with expectancy for God to answer your prayer. After praying for the person, make sure you rejoice and thank the Lord for the incredible opportunity you had. This is key for your next divine opportunity and for greater breakthrough!

Chapter 7

BECOMING A SUPERNATURAL SHOPPER

Supernatural Shopping

Every shopping experience can be an opportunity to see a life changed. Many times, we are praying for opportunities for God to use us, not realizing that the person next to us in aisle 5 needs a miracle in his or her body.

In this chapter, we'll discover that being a supernatural shopper is more than buying things that are on sale. Jesus purchased and paid for people's sin and sickness at full price. Being a supernatural shopper is being aware of His presence and the free gift of salvation, healing, and deliverance that He wants to give to other shoppers around you.

Power and Authority

Often when we are in a conference or a church setting, we may feel the presence of God in a tangible way. We may feel like anything is possible. Other times, as we are out in the community shopping, we may not feel anything. We want to move in power, but we don't feel it.

There Is a Difference Between Moving in Power and Moving in Authority

Often when you move in power, you may feel the manifestation of God's presence on you as well as moving through you. When you don't feel the tangible power and presence of God all over you, you can choose to move in the authority you have as a believer instead. Operating in power is best described as riding a spiritual wave, while operating out of authority is similar to creating a wave.

Authority is what opens the door for the power of God to flow through you. If you don't feel the power of God, you can invite God's power into the situation by stepping out in the authority that He has given you. Remind yourself who you are and who Christ is in you. Take a step of faith through the authority you have as a believer:

> *You did not choose Me, but I chose you and appointed you that you should go and bear fruit, and that your fruit should remain, that whatever you ask the Father in My name He may give you. These things I command you, that you love one another* (John 15:16-17).

As a disciple of Jesus, we have been given power and authority to do the works that He has called us to do:

> *Then He called His twelve disciples together and gave them power and authority over all demons, and to cure diseases. He sent them to preach the kingdom of God and to heal the sick* (Luke 9:1-2).

Hosting His Presence

Hosting the presence of God is about becoming aware of His love for us and for others around us. Hosting God's presence is what allows us to carry Heaven's environment with us wherever we go. People in grocery stores are not just hungry for natural food but for spiritual food and encounters as well. We have an opportunity to host Heaven's environment and bring healing, miracles, and life-changing God encounters into people's lives while we shop for our food.

Even though we are busy shopping, we can host His presence by turning the affection of our heart toward Him. As we're pushing our shopping cart down the aisle, we can simply remember what God has done in us and through us in our past. Thankfulness and worship invite the presence of God into our environment. Worship does not always need words or music; it's simply a position of the heart. It prepares a place for God to inhabit. If you want God's presence to inhabit your heart and mind while you are shopping, make room for Him by giving your time, your thoughts, and your worship.

Hosting God's presence activates the supernatural power of the Holy Spirit who lives in you. As you are pushing your cart down the aisle, you may get a word of knowledge or a prophetic word, or an overwhelming compassion for another shopper around you. This is a natural overflow of hosting God's presence while you are shopping. Learning to host God's presence, no matter where you are and what you are doing throughout the day, is an important key to supernatural ministry.

Look for the "Blue Light Special"

When we're hosting the presence of God by turning our hearts to Him, we find that God highlights people around us. It may be as if there is a light shining on them in the spiritual realm. When this happens, God has a special encounter for that individual. Many times as I have been shopping and I've turned my heart's affection to the Lord, people have been highlighted to me. As I've walked up to them and shared what the Lord has placed on my heart for them, their life has been radically impacted.

You know someone is highlighted to you when they just seem to stand out for some reason. Maybe you are walking through the grocery store and you keep noticing a specific person who seems to draw your eye. There does not seem to be any obvious reason. This may be because God is shining His light on them, waiting for you to recognize it so that you can help them encounter Jesus. Or maybe a person reminds you of someone from your past or your present. But as you are looking at them, you can't figure out what it is about them that reminds you. Recognize this as a divine opportunity for God to intervene in their life.

> Maybe you are walking through the grocery store and you keep noticing a specific person who seems to draw your eye. This may be because God is shining His light on them, waiting for you to recognize it so that you can help them encounter Jesus.

Practical Steps to Becoming a Supernatural Shopper

1. Take a minute or two of your time to ask and receive words of knowledge from the Holy Spirit and then write them down on your shopping list. I have included a shopping list with spaces for words of knowledge. Try to fill in every area with at least two or more.

2. After receiving words of knowledge from the Holy Spirit, fill in the rest of your shopping list with the groceries you need.

3. While driving or walking to the store, have a heart of expectation that God is going to do something supernatural through you.

4. Prepare your heart by turning your heart's affections toward the Lord before you even go in the store.

5. When you are in the store, relax and be yourself. Remind yourself that you are just shopping but now it is supernatural because you have partnered with the Holy Spirit.

6. Smile! You are more attractive this way. And the joy of the Lord is your strength.

7. While shopping, look for the "blue light specials" and for those that might be on your shopping list. When you see someone who looks like he or she might be on your list, approach the person and introduce yourself. Explain that before you came to the store, you asked Jesus who He wanted to love in a special way and that you wrote down on your shopping list some words that might mean something to the person.

8. Remember to be sensitive to what is going on in your body, emotions, and thoughts. Often, the Holy Spirit will give you words of knowledge even as you are in the store. These words of knowledge might not be written on your shopping list. That is okay.

9. While shopping, look for people who you know need healing or encouraging words. You can often tell who they are by the expression on people's faces.

10. For an easy way to introduce Jesus to someone (especially clerks, tellers, and even waiters or waitresses at restaurants) try asking, "Has anyone told you today that Jesus loves you, and has a plan for your life?" That question automatically requires an answer, which opens up an opportunity to share the Gospel.

11. As you are talking to people, pull on Heaven. Expect God to give you prophetic insight into their life as well as words of knowledge. For more on this, refer to Chapter 9.

Supernatural Shopping List

On this supernatural shopping list, adapted from Kevin Dedmon's Treasure Map in his book, *The Ultimate Treasure Hunt,* you'll find five areas that you can ask the Holy Spirit to reveal in order to lead you to people who will have God encounters:[1]

1. The names of those He wants to love in a special way.

2. What this person looks like and clothes he or she might be wearing.

3. The location or aisle of the store where the person will be.

4. Areas in the body that need healing.

5. The unusual things that point to the person that the Holy Spirit has picked out for you to love.

Questions to Ponder

1. How does becoming a supernatural shopper change the way you view shopping? How does it change the way you view evangelism?

_____

_____

_____

_____

2. What are some new ways you can bring God into other activities and errands you already do each day?

_____

_____

_____

_____

3. How does hosting the presence of God while shopping create opportunities for lives to be transformed around you?

_____

_____

_____

_____

Questions for Group Discussion

1. When God highlighted someone to you in the past, how did you respond? What would you do differently now?

_____

_____

_____

_____

2. What is the difference between moving in power and moving in authority?

_____

_____

_____

_____

3. How are you using the power and authority that Jesus has given you?

_____

_____

_____

_____

Life Application

During your next shopping opportunity, get filled with God's presence and be looking for God's "blue-light specials". Ask God for divine appointments to release His power through you while you are shopping.

Endnote

1. Kevin Dedmon, *The Ultimate Treasure Hunt: The Ultimate Guide to Supernatural Evangelism Through Supernatural Encounters* (Shippensburg, PA: Destiny Image Publishers, 2007).

Chapter 8

HOW TO LEAD SOMEONE TO THE LORD

The Holy Spirit Works to Reveal Jesus to Individuals

Many people have faith to see others healed, but might not have faith that God can use them to see someone get saved. The word *salvation* means "saved, healed and delivered." It comes from the Greek word *sozo*.[1] When one receives Jesus Christ into their heart, they step out of darkness and into light.

We often think that leading someone to the Lord is a difficult or complicated thing to do. When we partner with the Holy Spirit, what we're really doing is allowing the Spirit of Truth that lives inside of us to move through us and reveal truth to them. Jesus is the truth.

John 16:8 says, *"And when He has come, He will convict the world of sin, and of righteousness, and of judgment."* The Holy Spirit is the person who brings conviction of sin, not us. No one can be saved apart from the moving of the Holy Spirit and from the divine realization that one needs to be forgiven of their sins and reconciled to God. The Holy Spirit not only convicts us, but He also empowers us to repent. Not only does He empower us to repent (change the way we think), but He also empowers us to live a victorious life.

The Holy Spirit brings the conviction—not you! It's important that we know this as well as what to communicate to people. For example, in John 3:16, we know that *"God so loved the world that He gave His only begotten Son, that whoever believes in Him should not perish but have everlasting life."* Often we see the power of God touch people. It's very easy to lead people to Jesus because of the moving of the Holy Spirit. The Holy Spirit is aware of the desire in Heaven that none perish but all receive life through Jesus (see 2 Pet. 3:9).

Styles of Evangelism

There are many styles of evangelism being used today. Here are just a few, which I'll explain in more detail:

- ▶ Friendship evangelism
- ▶ Method presentation evangelism
- ▶ Prophetic arts evangelism
- ▶ Fire and brimstone evangelism
- ▶ Tracts

Friendship Evangelism

This can be very effective in business settings or at school. Essentially, you are building trust in an individual's life and heart, which gives you an ability to influence them. Often in friendship evangelism, discipleship comes naturally because of the heart connection and the trust factor.

Sometimes, those who have ministered in friendship evangelism come from a conservative Christian background where supernatural power may not be utilized. However, friendship evangelism partnered with the supernatural power of God is highly effective.

Method/Presentation Evangelism

This style of evangelism is often based on a method of presenting the Gospel. When we present the Gospel with love, the Gospel manifests. One method involves asking an unsaved person a question such as, "Do you know what it means to be born again?" The person may say no. Then you might say, "Do you mind if I explain it to you?" So you would tell them that in John chapter 3, Jesus tells us we must be born again. This style presents biblical truths from the Bible so that people will recognize the truth and want salvation. Presentation evangelism is also very effective when combined with a supernatural demonstration of the word that is being presented. In other words, you are not just teaching, you are demonstrating with power. If you present Jesus as the Healer, He will heal. If you present Him as the Savior, He will save. When you present Him and His nature, He will show up the way you declare Him to be:

> *For our gospel did not come to you in word only, but also in power, and in the Holy Spirit and in much assurance, as you know what kind of men we were among you for your sake* (1 Thessalonians 1:5).

Prophetic Arts Evangelism

Jesus is the creator of the universe. He used His imagination to first picture the universe, and then He created it. When He created humanity, He also gave us the power of divine imagination. This is what enables us to paint, sing, act, and dance.

He put a desire for creativity in the heart of every person. Prophetic arts evangelism, such as prophetic paintings or dramas, are a powerful way to awaken the supernatural creativity that may be dormant in an unsaved person's heart. When this creativity is awakened through this style of evangelism, their hearts open to the reality of the Creator.

Just as the Holy Spirit hovered over the earth during Creation, He hovers over the arts, wanting to awaken people's hearts through divine creativity. This style of evangelism is just another unique way to supernaturally reach people's hearts as the Holy Spirit awakens them through the arts.

Fire and Brimstone Evangelism

Fire and brimstone evangelism focuses more on an individual's sin condition than on the person. It's typically more fear-based than love-based.

Perhaps you've seen a person holding up a sign on a busy street corner shouting, "Repent! You are going to hell!" This is not often effective. I've never yet seen anyone positively impacted by this style of evangelism. However, I've seen many people upset by it and who have labeled Christians as people who are prideful, arrogant, and know-it-alls. I don't recommend this style. Love demonstrated with action is far more powerful and effective. Jesus never held up a sign. His life was the sign. These are not the signs He mentioned in Mark 16 that should follow our lives.

Tracts

Sometimes people in our culture hand out tracts either because they have a passion to reach people through the written word, or they are afraid to speak God's word because they simply don't know how. There is nothing wrong with using tracts, but it should not be our only style of evangelism. In our Western culture, I have sometimes seen people hide behind their tracts. The people handing out tracts may be motivated by fear—they may feel that God wants them to share the Gospel, but they don't know how. In this manual, you are learning new styles and methods of evangelism, not as an event but as a normal part of your life.

Recently I was in a grocery store and was getting ready to pay for my food. I asked the cashier, "Has anyone told you today that Jesus loves you?" She said, "No. However, some people recently gave me a tract." She then told me that the very fact that someone looked at her and communicated verbally to her, heart to heart, that Jesus loved her impacted her more than a tract did.

Foundational Scriptures of Salvation

Below are some foundational scriptures of salvation you should memorize. You'll find these very useful when you are talking to someone who wants to know Jesus in a personal way. Other salvation scriptures can be found in Appendix A at the end of this book.

If you confess with your mouth the Lord Jesus and believe in your heart that God has raised Him from the dead, you will be saved. For with the heart one believes unto righteousness, and with the mouth confession is made unto salvation (Romans 10:9-10).

But as many as received Him, to them He gave the right to become children of God, to those who believe in His name (John 1:12).

For God so loved the world that He gave His only begotten Son, that whoever believes in Him should not perish but have everlasting life. For God did not send His Son into the world to condemn the world, but that the world through Him might be saved (John 3:16-17).

Most assuredly, I say to you, the hour is coming, and now is, when the dead will hear the voice of the Son of God; and those who hear will live (John 5:25).

And when He has come, He will convict the world of sin, and of righteousness, and of judgment (John 16:8).

But when the Helper comes, whom I shall send to you from the Father, the Spirit of truth who proceeds from the Father, He will testify of Me. And you also will bear witness, because you have been with Me from the beginning (John 15:26-27).

Partnering With the Holy Spirit

The Holy Spirit supernaturally empowers you for evangelism. When you partner with Him, He makes it easy to do evangelism because He wants to do the hard part for you.

> The Holy Spirit supernaturally empowers you for evangelism. When you partner with Him, He makes it easy to do evangelism because He wants to do the hard part for you.

The Holy Spirit:

- Reveals Jesus Christ to the unsaved.
- Reveals God's love and acceptance to them.
- Opens up their heart to believe that Jesus died on the cross for all their sins and sicknesses and that He rose again on the third day.
- Empowers them to confess their need for Jesus, as well as confess their sins that have separated them from relationship with God so that they can be forgiven.

Keys to Unlock the Hearts of Humanity

As you present the Gospel, these are some key things you can focus on to unlock people's hearts in one-on-one conversations:

▶ Focus on Heaven.

▶ Focus on restored relationship between the unsaved and God.

▶ Focus on God's ability to transform identities.

▶ Focus on the result of Salvation: an empowered, Spirit-filled believer.

Focus on Heaven

Heaven is our model. Our responsibility as a believer is to demonstrate Heaven through encounters to those who have a broken relationship with God through sin.

As you are presenting the Gospel, it's important that your focus is on Heaven. How you represent Jesus to the individual will often determine their ability to experience Him. If I minister to a fractured person in a harsh way, their ability to receive God's love will be greatly hindered. If I discern that this person is fractured, and I speak to them in a loving voice of honor and care, their hearts are more likely to be receptive. As we focus on Heaven, we see God's redemption. We see the potential and the destiny that God has for the people we are speaking to. Despite all the things that might be wrong with them, we know God's love is greater than any sin condition they may have.

Restored Relationship

The goal of evangelism is not for someone just to repeat a prayer, but for him or her to understand it is about a relationship with God. Remember that the Father's heart is about relationship with one another and us. In the world that we live in, we see broken relationships and broken families. The person you are speaking with may be from one of those families. God has a family, and God has children. His heart is to reconcile His children into His family.

The answer to a person's sin is restored relationship with God. The word *righteous* in the Greek means "right relationship with

God."[2] It's important for people to know that they can be reconciled to God, that they can have a one-on-one relationship because the Holy Spirit is on earth to reconcile them to the Father.

> *Therefore, if anyone is in Christ, he is a new creation; old things have passed away; behold, all things have become new. Now all things are of God, who has reconciled us to Himself through Jesus Christ, and has given us the ministry of reconciliation, that is, that God was in Christ reconciling the world to Himself, not imputing their trespasses to them, and has committed to us the word of reconciliation. Now then, we are ambassadors for Christ, as though God were pleading through us: we implore you on Christ's behalf, be reconciled to God. For He made Him who knew no sin to be sin for us, that we might become the righteousness of God in Him* (2 Corinthians 5:17-21).

Transformed Identity

As you are sharing the Gospel with people, one of the exciting things you get to share with them is their new identity. When someone receives Jesus into their heart, they receive relationship, which opens up a whole new world to them—the Kingdom of God. This world is full of experiences: getting to know their Creator and experiencing the love of their Father. The Father's love will transcend every other encounter they have ever had prior to being born again. This encounter of love is an ongoing encounter, full of discoveries.

This relationship enables people to have encounters with God's love, which forms their identity. As people experience the powerful love of God, there is an explosion and an awakening in their hearts that helps people comprehend that they're forgiven.

Anyone, whether saved or unsaved, can expect the following to occur when they have power encounters with the love of God:

- ▶ The love of God produces confidence.

- ▶ The love of God reveals your identity.

- ▶ The love of God creates a sense of belonging in God's family.

- ▶ The love of God empowers people to have access to the Father.

- ▶ The love of God enables us to love other people.

- ▶ The love of God replaces anger with love.

- ▶ The love of God removes depression, anxiety, and fear.

When a person receives Jesus, His light peels away the darkness that has held them captive for so long. Jesus snatches their life out of a realm of darkness, and takes them through a one-step program into the light. A person who opens his or her heart to Jesus is now on the journey of the Christian life and their identity has changed from sinner to saint. Paul spoke to the Ephesian church as saints, not sinners saved by grace (see Eph. 1).

Our "lens," the way that we see things, often determines how we live. If I believe that I'm a sinner saved by grace, it's easy for me to revert back to my old lifestyle of sin because my identity hasn't changed. But if I believe that I'm a saint because of His love and grace, that Kingdom mindset changes my identity and empowers me to be a victorious believer.

It is also important for us to see the newly saved as saints, not forgiven sinners. This enables you to look for the gold inside them, and to see their God-given potential. Then you can express to them who they truly are in Christ, and you can help them recognize that their identity has changed, which empowers them to live as saints. God sees those who have given their hearts to Him as saints, and, as we acknowledge their identity as saints, they step into an empowering culture.

Empowered, Spirit-filled Believers

Years ago in South Africa, we prayed for a family who all received Jesus into their hearts. One of the younger brothers had a problem in his stomach and needed prayer for healing. I asked his older brother, "Would you like to pray for your brother? You just received Jesus into your heart. And the Lord Jesus hears you just as much as He hears me. It's normal for believers to move in power. So go ahead and lay your hand on his stomach and command all the pain to leave."

As he did that, all the pain left his brother's body. This story illustrates to us that as soon as a person becomes a believer, they can operate in the Kingdom and demonstrate God's power in miracles, signs, and wonders.

The ABCs of Christianity

The unsaved person needs to:

► Admit s/he is a sinner. Admit there is sin that is holding him or her back from relationship with God. (In doing so, the person is giving up the sin that holds him or her her back from relationship.)

► Believe that Jesus is the Son of God and that He died and rose again.

► Confess Him as Lord and renounce anything that has separated him or her from a relationship with God.

ADMIT Being a Sinner

The Holy Spirit reveals to people their need for a Savior. When people understand that their sin is blocking them from relationship with the Father, they will recognize their need for a Savior. Jesus is the Savior who broke down the wall of separation, which keeps people distant from the Father. As the Holy Spirit moves through you, people will be convicted of their sins and develop a hunger to know the Father and have a relationship with Him through Jesus Christ.

BELIEVE That Jesus Is the Son of God and That He Died and Rose Again

The Holy Spirit empowers people to believe that Jesus is the Son of God and that Jesus loves them and paid the price for their sin by shedding His own blood on the cross. The Holy Spirit also empowers them to believe that they can have a relationship with Jesus and know Him personally. He brings a supernatural awareness into their heart that their life can be different through Jesus Christ.

When we are presenting the Gospel to people, it is the Holy Spirit who empowers them to believe the Good News. The Holy Spirit deposits seeds of truth that explode in people's hearts, which creates faith to believe that Jesus Christ paid for their sins. When you are partnering with the Holy Spirit, He will work on the hearts of people to reveal their need for a Savior.

> Now when they heard this, they were cut to the heart, and said to Peter and the rest of the apostles, "Men and brethren, what shall we do?" Then Peter said to them, "Repent, and let every one of you be baptized in the name of Jesus Christ for the remission of sins; and you shall receive the gift of the Holy Spirit. For the promise is to you and to your children, and to all who are afar off, as many as the Lord our God will call" (Acts 2:37-39).

CONFESS and Renounce

The Holy Spirit shines a light of truth on their sin and empowers them to confess the sins for which all need forgiveness. In that moment of being born again, He reminds them of past sin and shows how that has distanced them from God. As the Holy Spirit brings past sins to remembrance, He enables them to confess those sins to Jesus who will then cleanse us with His blood. Freedom and forgiveness come through confession.

The Holy Spirit not only empowers us to confess our sins, He wants us to live in freedom. He empowers us to forsake our sins as we renounce them. Confession is admitting sin; renouncing is giving sin up. As we give our sins to Jesus, we are making room for Him to fill our heart with His presence. As He fills us, He naturally enables and empowers us to live without those sins. Because sin separates us from relationship with God, believers can have a continual, daily relationship with the Father, Son, and Holy Spirit because their sins have been forgiven.

Salvation Encounter

As I've mentioned before in this book, we shouldn't do anything based on a formula. However, many readers may want to have an example of how I might lead someone in a salvation prayer to start a relationship with Jesus.

Although it's different each time, I may have them pray something like this:

> *"Jesus, thank You for revealing Yourself to me. Thank You for dying on the cross for all my sins because You love me. I believe that You rose again from the dead and are alive. Today I give You all of my past sin. Please forgive me and come into my heart. I receive You as my Savior, my Healer, and my Deliverer. I renounce any other spirit that I have invited into my life because of hurt and pain. I command them to leave me right now in Jesus' name. Holy Spirit, come and fill me, transform me, and empower me to be like Jesus. I welcome You, Holy Spirit, to transform my life. Empower me to be a witness to tell others about the love of Jesus that I've experienced."*

At this point, I would pray for them to be baptized in the Holy Spirit. Then I'd ask them to thank Jesus for saving them and restoring their relationship with God.

Don't memorize this prayer! Salvation prayers should never be a formula. There are so many ways to lead someone to Jesus through prayer, it's just a matter of getting them into an encounter with Him, getting rid of the sin, and inviting Him into their heart so they are changed. Anything else you want to add to the prayer is only going to help the person, so go for it!

Salvation comes through an encounter, not just through prayer. As you are praying for others to receive Christ, the goal is that they will experience Christ and that their life will begin to be transformed.

After leading the person to the Lord, explain, "Just as Jesus has forgiven you of all your sins and does not remember them anymore, He asks us to extend that forgiveness to others. Is there anyone in your life you need to forgive?" They might say, "I don't know." Or they might say, "Yes."

If they say, "I don't know," ask if it would be okay to pray for the Holy Spirit to reveal to them if they have any unforgiveness toward anyone (see Chapter 6). If the person recognizes the need to forgive someone, lead in a similar prayer like you did in Chapter 6. After leading in a prayer of forgiveness, have the person invite the Holy Spirit to fill his or her heart with peace and joy as a replacement for the unforgiveness s/he was holding. Also explain, "As you live this life with Jesus, just as He is faithful and just to forgive you of all your sins when you confess them to Him, we should be faithful to forgive others who may hurt us. This will empower us to stay close to Jesus."

Ways to Present the Gospel

After introducing yourself to someone, if you feel you have rapport with him or her, say something like this: "Hey, do you mind if I ask you a question?" Wait for their response. "Do you know what it means to be born again?"

If they say yes, then ask them, "Have you ever been born again?" If they say no, ask them, "Do you mind if I explain to you what it means to be born again?"

If they say, "Okay," share the story in John chapter 3. Make it simple for them to understand. You can relate it to them like this:

> In John chapter 3, there was this religious leader named Nicodemus who came to Jesus one night. He had a lot of questions for Jesus. He claimed to know God but he didn't really know God at the time. After he asked Jesus a question, Jesus responded to Nicodemus and said something like this. "Nicodemus, you must be born again."
>
> This religious leader said to Jesus, "How can man be born when he is old? Can he enter into his mother's womb a second time?"
>
> Jesus explained to Nicodemus that flesh gives birth to flesh, and spirit gives birth to spirit. Being born again is a spiritual rebirth.

After explaining to them that being born again is not a physical birth but a supernatural birth, explain to them that God wants them to be called children of God. Explain John 1:12:

> *But as many as received Him, to them He gave the right to become children of God, to those who believe in His name.*

When individuals receive Jesus in their heart by faith, they are called children of God.

Romans 10:10 says that when we believe with our heart and confess with our mouth that Jesus Christ is Lord and that God raised Him from the dead, we shall be saved.

Another way to present the Gospel to someone is to ask him or her, "Has anyone given you an encouraging word today?" Wait for a response. As you are waiting, ask the Holy Spirit to give you an encouraging prophetic word for them. After you've given the prophetic word, explain to them that Jesus loves them and has a plan for their life. Ask them simply, "Have you ever had an experience with the presence of God before? Do you know Jesus personally? Would you like to experience His presence?"

What I like to do is ask them to hold their hands out palms facing up. As they do that, I place my hands above theirs in the air and pray a simple prayer: "Holy Spirit, reveal Jesus to them." Shortly after this, I ask them: "What are you feeling? What is happening in your heart?" Often people respond by describing feeling a presence all over them. This is a perfect time to explain the Gospel to them and to ask if they would like to receive Jesus Christ into their heart.

Another way is to ask them, "How do you deal with guilt and shame?" Wait for them to talk and explain. Then explain to them how you have dealt with guilt and shame. Another way you can phrase this is, "How do you deal with past failures in your life?" This is a great way to explain your own testimony and to present the Gospel.

There are other great ways to begin presenting the Gospel to people by asking them simple questions. You will discover others as the Holy Spirit leads you.

Discipleship in the Christian Lifestyle

After a person has received Jesus Christ into his or her heart, it's important that you rejoice with the person, encourage, and affirm that all his or her sins are forgiven. In God's sight, they are completely clean. This new believer is in right standing with Jesus and has now become a child of God. Spiritual children are moldable and open to what mature believers share with them. It's important that you sow truths into their hearts and lives because children need spiritual nutrients to grow and mature.

It's important that you point new believers in a direction where they can be fed spiritually. We don't want to overwhelm the person with a to-do list. Rather, we want to offer resources to the hungry Christian, as they're ready for it. A hungry person will define his or her own pace of learning.

Here are some ways new Christians can grow and mature.

Relationship

They need to be discipled and connected to other Christians. The first six months are crucial in new Christians' growth. During this time, they need to be connected and built up. They need to know and experience God's love for them, which will become the foundation for the rest of their Christian life.

Connection With a Good Church

You'll want to direct new Christians to a good church that preaches the solid truth of the Bible. It's also important for the believer to not try to be good, but to simply fall in love with Jesus. Lovers get more done than workers do!

Give Them a Bible and Start Them in the Gospel of John

Have new believers keep a journal and write down things that stick out to them in the Gospel of John, and what the Lord may be speaking to them about those things.

Encourage Them to Rid Their Lives of Hindrances

Encourage them to get rid of anything that might hinder their growth in a relationship with Jesus. For example, the Holy Spirit's ability to move in a believer's life can be hindered by bad music, bad magazines, harmful relationships, witchcraft, or drugs. Because they really want to grow, new Christians will be eager to get rid of things that hinder their growth plan.

The Power of Thankfulness

Teach them the power of thankfulness. As they thank God for their freedom from sin and their old lifestyle, they will grow and mature even more because thankfulness produces increase. This is a powerful Kingdom principle that will allow them to live as saints.

Prayer

Teach them the simplicity of prayer. It is conversation between them and God. And in conversation, there is always more than one person talking. God wants to hear what is on their mind. And God wants to tell them what is on His mind as well. Encourage them to listen for the voice of God.

Share Their Faith With Others

Have them share their faith and testimony with others by sharing what Jesus did in their lives. Sharing a testimony causes faith to explode in their life as they realize that they are no longer the person they used to be. They are a new creation, and the old things have passed away. Declaring this testimony to others will help them to continually remember this, as well as give others hope in the Gospel of Jesus Christ.

Relationship Tools for the New Christian

- Get alone with the Lord.
- Meditate on God's Word.
- Ask the Holy Spirit to reveal truths in the Scriptures.
- Look for things in the Bible that jump out to you.
- Take time to rest in God's presence.
- Ask Him plainly, "How do You see me?"
- Wait for Him to speak the answer.
- Write down what He is saying to you.
- Ask Him any questions that may be on your heart.

▶ Again, take some time to listen.

▶ Remember that God always wants to speak to you. That's why He sent His Son to restore us in relationship Him. Through Jesus, there is no distance. God is always near.

▶ Ask for the baptism of the Holy Spirit (see Acts 2).

▶ Ask Him for a prayer language through the gift of tongues.

▶ Ask the Holy Spirit, "Is there anything You would like to reveal to me today?" Write it down.

▶ Ask the Holy Spirit to show you any roadblocks in your life.

▶ If He shows you one, renounce it and ask for the Holy Spirit to empower you to be an overcomer.

▶ Ask the Holy Spirit to reveal God's love for others around you.

▶ Ask the Holy Spirit to empower you to be a witness to others throughout your daily life.

Questions to Ponder

1. How does having a Heavenly mindset affect the way I share the Gospel of the Kingdom with people?

   _____

   _____

   _____

   _____

2. Why is it important to be sensitive to the Holy Spirit and how He's leading me to share with others?

   _____

   _____

   _____

   _____

3. Why is focusing on restored relationship more powerful than focusing on someone's sin?

   _____

   _____

   _____

   _____

4. How does the Holy Spirit convict someone of his or her sins?

   _____

   _____

   _____

   _____

Questions for Group Discussion

1. What style of evangelism have you been accustomed to prior to reading this book? How does it differ from the style presented here?

    _____

    _____

    _____

2. What is the fruit of "fire and brimstone" evangelism? What is the fruit of the "Kingdom" evangelism style presented here?

    _____

    _____

    _____

Life Application

With great expectation, look for people who need a restored relationship with God to share the Gospel of the Kingdom with. Talk to at least five people this week and ask them, "Has anyone given you an encouraging word today?"

Endnotes

1. James Strong, *Strong's Exhaustive Concordance of the Bible* (Peabody, MA: Hendrickson Publishers, 1988), *sozo*, #4982.

2. *Ibid.*, righteous, #6662.

Chapter 9

WORDS OF KNOWLEDGE

What Is a Word of Knowledge?

A word of knowledge is one of the nine gifts of the Spirit listed in First Corinthians 12:4-11. A word of knowledge is divine revelation into someone's life, usually a specific detail that you could not have known unless the Holy Spirit revealed it to you. People sometimes confuse words of knowledge with prophetic words or words of wisdom. A word of knowledge is a specific detail about another person's life, either past or present. It is immediately verifiable, unlike prophetic words, which relate to the future and are confirmed when they occur.

Once, while I was leading a meeting, I got a word of knowledge that someone in the meeting had planned to commit suicide two months earlier. I heard God say to me that if this person laid her hands on her stomach, God would break off the spirit of suicide. After the meeting, a young lady came up to me and told me that three months ago she'd been brutally raped. Two months ago, she had planned to commit suicide. As she laid her hand on her stomach, the Father healed her heart completely of all the pain she had been carrying for the past three months.

God can give words of knowledge to believers for many reasons. He may tell you that a person needs healing from a specific pain, sickness, or disease. He may also use a word of knowledge to tell somebody that He knows them and is near to them. When somebody hears you say something about them that you couldn't possibly have known without divine revelation, it opens up their heart to realize that God is real and that He loves them.

God may give you directions through words of knowledge such as when God told Ananias to go find Saul of Tarsus in Acts chapter 9. Let's look at this passage. Note all the details that God gave Ananias:

> Now there was a certain disciple at Damascus named Ananias; and to him the Lord said in a vision, "Ananias." And he said, "Here I am, Lord."
>
> So the Lord said to him, "Arise and go to the street called Straight, and inquire at the house of Judas for one called Saul of Tarsus, for behold, he is praying. And in a vision he has seen a man named Ananias coming in and putting his hand on him, so that he might receive his sight."
>
> Then Ananias answered, "Lord, I have heard from many about this man, how much harm he has done to Your saints in Jerusalem. And here he has authority from the chief priests to bind all who call on Your name." But the Lord said to him, "Go, for he is a chosen vessel of Mine to bear My name before Gentiles, kings, and the children of Israel. For I will show him how many things he must suffer for My name's sake."
>
> And Ananias went his way and entered the house; and laying his hands on him he said, "Brother Saul, the Lord Jesus, who appeared to you on the road as you came, has sent me that you may receive your sight and be filled with the Holy Spirit." Immediately there fell from his eyes

something like scales, and he received his sight at once; and he arose and was baptized.

So when he had received food, he was strengthened. Then Saul spent some days with the disciples at Damascus (Acts 9:10-19).

Ananias knew the following things:

1. Saul was staying at the house of Judas.

2. The house was on a street called Straight.

3. He was to ask for Saul of Tarsus.

4. Saul had been praying.

5. Saul was blind.

6. The way to release healing to Saul.

7. Saul had an encounter with Jesus on the road to Damascus.

Jesus also got many words of knowledge during His ministry. For example, He had a very memorable encounter with Nathaniel:

The following day Jesus wanted to go to Galilee, and He found Philip and said to him, "Follow Me." Now Philip was from Bethsaida, the city of Andrew and Peter. Philip found Nathanael and said to him, "We have found Him of whom Moses in the law, and also the prophets, wrote— Jesus of Nazareth, the son of Joseph."

And Nathanael said to him, "Can anything good come out of Nazareth?"

Philip said to him, "Come and see."

Jesus saw Nathanael coming toward Him, and said of him, "Behold, an Israelite indeed, in whom is no deceit!"

Nathanael said to Him, "How do You know me?"

Jesus answered and said to him, "Before Philip called you, when you were under the fig tree, I saw you."

Nathanael answered and said to Him, "Rabbi, You are the Son of God! You are the King of Israel!" (John 1:43-49).

Jesus had divine revelation about Nathanael before He met him.

1. Jesus was able to recognize Nathanael the first time He saw him because He'd seen him through a divine revelation.

2. Jesus saw Nathanael standing under a fig tree.

3. Jesus knew that Nathanael was a man of character and integrity.

Notice Nathanael's reaction to Jesus' words of knowledge. Nathanael answered Jesus by saying excitedly, "You are the Son of God!" This word of knowledge affected Nathanael so much that he immediately gave his heart to Jesus.

Words of Knowledge in Action

When you receive a word of knowledge about someone's life, which is then confirmed, it releases faith in your heart that you are hearing from God. It also releases faith in the atmosphere.

The word of knowledge in action is a power encounter that points people to Jesus. Words of knowledge can come for various reasons:

▶ God knows everything about the person.

▶ They communicate God's love to the person so that they know that they are not alone and that God cares for them.

- ▶ They knock on the door to people's hearts.

- ▶ They explode faith into the atmosphere.

- ▶ They bring emotional and physical healing.

In the Old Testament, the only people who moved in the gift of words of knowledge were prophets. Now, this gift from the Holy Spirit is available to every believer. The gift of the word of knowledge will empower you to speak to people's hearts supernaturally as God reveals details about them that you couldn't possibly have known otherwise. I've found this to be one of the most effective gifts for evangelism. When moving in this gift, it can create an atmosphere of faith. It opens people's hearts when they have an encounter through the gift of a word of knowledge.

A person who has just experienced a word of knowledge will often say, "How did you know that? Who told you that?" This opens up the door for you to explain that it was God who just spoke to you, and He has good things to say about that person's life because He loves them. It also opens the door to a miracle as you say, "God told me about your knee pain because He loves you and wants to heal you. Can I pray for you to be healed right now?"

Because they already realize a miracle has occurred (you knew something about them by divine means), they'll want the rest of the miracle (supernatural healing). Words of knowledge open doors in the spiritual realm for people to receive their healing because when the word is released faith is supernaturally released in the atmosphere:

> *Meanwhile praying also for us, that God would open to us a door for the word, to speak the mystery of Christ, for which I am also in chains, that I may make it manifest, as I ought to speak* (Colossians 4:3-4).

Often you may receive a word of knowledge without knowing that it is a word of knowledge. God has given us spiritual senses that need to be trained by the Holy Spirit and exercised frequently by us.

Words of Knowledge for Healing

The first step should be to ask the Holy Spirit for the gift of words of knowledge. You can receive the gift directly from the Lord or indirectly from another person through an impartation. Impartation is a Kingdom way to give away gifts and grace from person to person. In Romans 1:11 Paul says, *"I long to see you that I may "impart" to you some spiritual gift, so that you may be established."* The word "impart" means to give, share, or distribute.[1]

Below are some ways (although not the only ways), you can get words of knowledge for healing.

1. *Feeling pain in your body that is not your pain*

I got my first word of knowledge while I was in line at an airport. As I was talking to a woman, my right ear began to hurt. I knew that this was not my pain. I asked her, "By any chance, do you have any pain in your right ear?" She said, "Yes," so I asked if I could pray for her. After praying, she was healed.

2. *Receiving a picture in your mind about a body part that may need healing*

When you ask for a word of knowledge, you may get a picture in your mind about a body part or location of someone's body that may need healing. If you don't know whom it's for, ask the Lord to show you.

3. *God highlighting someone or something to you*

As you are talking to someone (or maybe you see someone at a distance), you may notice a certain area of his or her body that seems to stick out to you. When your focus is drawn to a certain part of their body, this is called *highlighting*. This is a way that God can direct your attention to a healing. After I have responded to this word of knowledge, I have often seen people healed in the highlighted body part.

4. Hearing the Lord speak detailed things about someone's body

While talking to someone, you may hear the Lord speak something directly into your heart for a person's healing. Be sensitive to hear God's voice. He may bring Scriptures to remembrance on how He healed individuals.

5. Strong impressions

You will notice that when you get around certain people at times you may have impressions in your heart that they are in need of healing. You may recognize their need for healing by inner conviction or strong impressions. The person may not appear to be in need of healing, but by being sensitive to the Holy Spirit's impressions, you can recognize these words of knowledge to release healing.

6. Remembering a previous testimony about healing

As you go about your day, you might remember a previous healing that occurred days, weeks, or even months ago. That testimony you are remembering is often a summoning to another miracle. The testimony of Jesus Christ is the spirit of prophecy (see Rev. 19:10).

7. Prophetic dreams

I had a dream in which I was ministering to a woman who needed healing in her body. The next morning I was preaching at a juvenile hall and I remembered the dream. I did not know which person it was for, but as I looked over the young prisoners, there was one young lady who was highlighted to me. As I asked her to stand, the Lord began to show me things about her life. As I ministered, God brought healing to her.

Revelation, Interpretation, and Application

When you have received a word of knowledge, you receive revelation from the Holy Spirit about a person's situation. Interpretation may be necessary when you don't know what the revelation (word of knowledge) means or who it applies to. There may be times when you need to ask the Holy Spirit for interpretation. Do this and then listen and wait for it. Application is the way in which you practically go about delivering the revelation. Words of knowledge may not always be delivered the same way. If the Holy Spirit has not shown you how to deliver the word of knowledge, ask and wait for Him to reveal it to you.

Getting Activated in Words of Knowledge

If you are not willing to take a risk to get activated in words of knowledge, you will never be able to step out in this gift. Words of knowledge, like most other spiritual gifts, require faith in action, which requires risk.

As you wake up in the morning, ask the Holy Spirit, "Is there anyone I'm going to meet today that You would like to speak to?" Have a pen and paper ready to write down anything He reveals to you. For example, if the Lord gives you a name like Bob, press in for more details. Ask the Lord, "How old is Bob? What is his age range? What does he look like? Where will I see him? What might he need prayer for?" Ask the Lord for detailed, specific words of knowledge about anything He reveals to you. The first revelation may be an invitation for you to press in for a higher level, more detailed word of knowledge.

Whenever somebody calls you on the phone whom you don't know, ask the Holy Spirit to give you insight into that person's life. This works great with telemarketers! A few years ago, I had a female telemarketer call me. As she was talking, I asked the Holy Spirit to show me things about her life. After she finished, I asked if I could share a couple of things with her. She said yes. I shared things about her and her family. This touched her heart so much; she wanted to know who told me! I told her it was Jesus Christ who told me. She was so impacted with God's love, she was crying over the phone because of this encounter with God's love. Even over the phone, you can give people powerful encounters with God using words of knowledge.

When you are at a stoplight or stuck in traffic, ask the Holy Spirit if He has anything to say to the car next to you. I have seen many people touched at stoplights and in traffic as the Holy Spirit give me words of knowledge! But the only way I got to have these amazing ministry times was by being willing to take a risk and step out in faith.

As you eat out in restaurants, ask the Holy Spirit to give you words of knowledge for your waiter or waitress. When the waiter comes around, be yourself and build rapport. Ask them if the word of knowledge makes sense to them. You can say, "Hey, I was praying and I had a sense that you might have pain in your body. By any chance, do you have pain in your right shoulder?" This question will require an answer, either a yes or a no. It's a great way for you to step out in faith in public. If they think you are weird, explain to them that you are learning to hear God's voice. Most people in public are happy to help anyone who is practicing to hear God's voice.

When you are around large groups of people such as in a retail store or a supermarket, ask the Holy Spirit to highlight people to you who need healing in their body. After He shows you someone, ask Him to give you more insight. Ask Him what it is that they need healing from and how long they have had the problem. Then press even deeper into their life and ask God to reveal to you their name and about their family. Every word of knowledge is like a door. It opens up to another realm. Beyond that door are many other doors.

Just as doors lead to more doors, details lead to more details. The only way to open up more details is to press in for more.

> If you want high-level, detailed words of knowledge, you have to be willing to take a risk. Taking risk takes you places you've never been before. Stepping out in words of knowledge that are unfamiliar to you may feel like stepping on foreign ground, but the more you tread on that ground, the more familiar it becomes.

If you want high-level, detailed words of knowledge, you have to be willing to take a risk. Risk takes you places you've never been before. Stepping out in words of knowledge that are unfamiliar to you may feel like stepping on foreign ground, but the more you tread on that ground, the more familiar it becomes.

As you are stepping out and taking risks, you may not feel very confident. But confidence is like a muscle. The more you exercise it, the more you grow. Confidence will come as you continue stepping out and taking risks. It will get easier.

Questions to Ponder

1. How is a word of knowledge different from a prophetic word?

    _____

    _____

    _____

    _____

2. What ways does the Holy Spirit speak through the word of knowledge?

    _____

    _____

    _____

    _____

3. How does the gift of the word of knowledge become an effective tool for evangelism?

    _____

    _____

    _____

    _____

4. What is the difference between revelation and interpretation?

    _____

    _____

    _____

    _____

Questions for Group Discussion

1. Why is risk a huge factor for getting and giving words of knowledge?

   _____

   _____

   _____

Group Activity

In your small group, divide up in pairs. Each person should ask God to show him or her something about the other person. Then deliver whatever God reveals to you, even if you don't know what it means. And remember, each person is looking for the gold!

Example: If I'm praying for someone I might see a picture in my mind. I might say, "I see a red house with a brown car in front and three cats. And I see a neighbor with a dog." Then I would ask them, "Does any of that make sense to you?"

Life Application

When you wake up, take a pen and paper and ask the Lord whom you are going to meet today. Ask for key details and write them down. Throughout your day, look for people who may be on your list. However, God can even point people out to you who aren't on your list so you always need to be aware of what God is saying.

Endnote

1. James Strong, *Strong's Exhaustive Concordance of the Bible* (Peabody, MA: Hendrickson publishers, 1988), impart, #3330.

Chapter 10

PROPHETIC EVANGELISM

What Is Prophecy?

Prophecy is one of the nine gifts of the Spirit listed in First Corinthians chapter 12. Paul encourages us to seek gifts, but especially prophecy. To prophesy is to call out the gold in people around you. Prophecy is a gift that cannot be earned, but must be received freely by faith.

Consider yourself to be a gold miner. As you prophesy, you will discover the heart of God for people's lives. It does not take a prophetic gift to find dirt (sin) in people's lives. It takes a prophetic gift to see the gold in people.

God created greatness in every person. But sometimes our past dirt (mistakes) determines how we see ourselves. But God does not focus on our dirt. Prophetic individuals have the opportunity to call out the gold (greatness) in a person's life when all that is visible to the natural eye is dirt (mistakes).

Pursue love, and desire spiritual gifts, but especially that you may prophesy. For he who speaks in a tongue does not speak to men but to God, for no one understands him; however, in the spirit he speaks mysteries. But he who prophesies speaks edification and exhortation and comfort to men (1 Corinthians 14:1-3).

Paul teaches us that prophecy is for edification, exhortation, and comfort. These things come from the heart of God to deposit life into the person who's receiving the word.

As you are learning to prophesy, it's important that you do not prophesy out of your emotions. Learn to prophesy from the heart of the Father. We may hear someone give a prophetic word that sounds like, "I see this cloud over you and it's very dark. I see that you are in this season of your life where you feel spiritually heavy. The season is going to last for six months and your family will feel shaken by it. But don't worry, after six months, your family is going to be healthier in God."

That's not an encouraging word! If you or your family received that word, that would not encourage you! That would not build you up. If you see something negative in someone's life, it is your job to prophesy a positive solution for the negative, or to refrain from prophesying at all. You should also stop speaking when God stops speaking. The motivation of prophetic evangelism should be love. Remember, love opens up the door for you to hear God's voice and to speak what He is saying. God is always speaking because His name is the Word of God.

Love opens up the door for you to hear God's voice and to speak what He is saying. God is always speaking because His name is the Word of God.

The Difference Between a Prophet and Someone Who Prophesies

Christ gave five gifts to the Church body, and a prophet is one of these gifts. A prophet's primary job is to equip the saints for the work of ministry through teaching and to impart the grace and anointing for the prophetic gift on a believer's life. Someone who does not occupy the office of a prophet can still prophesy using a gift of prophecy that is given by the Holy Spirit as mentioned in First Corinthians chapter 14.

God never intended prophecy to be limited to just the prophets. Paul tells us in First Corinthians 14:1 to pursue love but desire spiritual gifts, especially prophecy. Prophecy is for all believers, young and old.

The Power of Prophecy in Evangelism

When people hear about how God sees them, it opens up their heart to hear more. Prophetic evangelism is about communicating the heart of the Father to His children. This revelation of God's heart builds a natural hunger in people to want to know more about Him.

Recently one of our teams was at a football game doing prophetic evangelism. One of the team members prophesied over an individual. His life was so impacted that others around him asked the team for prophetic words as well. After hearing what God had said about this young man, they all wanted to know what God thought about them!

The people around this young man saw the power of God touch him through the prophetic and they were hungry to experience the same power.

But prophetic insight must be used properly. We don't want to give words like, "I see a black cloud over your life. Your family is going to leave you in the next week. Even your dog is going to leave you! But don't worry, just like Job, God will restore everything to you seven times greater after this season." This bad prophetic word creates fear and anxiety and gives a false representation of the heart of God. Even though the word ends positively, it still has negative elements in it that are not encouraging. Only give encouraging words.

If you see or feel anything negative as you are prophesying, speak the life of Heaven instead. Declare the opposite. For example, "I see transformation in your life. God wants to touch your family. God even wants to heal your dog." Our words carry the power of life and death.

> *Death and life are in the power of the tongue* (Proverbs 18:21).

> *There is one who speaks like the piercings of a sword, but the tongue of the wise promotes health* (Proverbs 12:18).

Prophetic evangelism should be motivated by love and honor and should bring edification, exhortation, and comfort to people. Most people out in the community will not understand what prophetic evangelism is. But everyone knows what an encouraging word is. Our job is to bring encouragement and life to the world around us.

The Holy Spirit will often give you prophetic insight into people's lives so you can see the gold in them. Prophetic evangelism is highly effective because it pierces the hearts of the lost and opens a door to the Father's love.

Receiving the Gift of Prophecy

There are different ways to receive the gift of prophecy. The first way is by asking the Holy Spirit for the gift. Or you can receive the gift through impartation from another person.

If you don't have the gift of prophecy, you can get it now from the Holy Spirit.

1. Ask the Holy Spirit to give you this gift of prophecy. As Matthew 7:7-8 says, *"Everyone who asks, receives."*

2. Say, "Holy Spirit, give me the gift of prophecy to encourage the Body of Christ and nonbelievers. I receive this gift in faith."

Practical Activation for Prophetic Evangelism

Get with a friend and practice prophesying over each other. Take a minute and ask the Holy Spirit, "What are You saying about John? What do You have to tell me that would encourage John right now?"

When you prophesy over someone, you may receive words for that person in different ways. Prophetic words may come to us in the same way that words of knowledge come to us (see Chapter 9).

When receiving a prophetic word for someone, it is important that you remember you can have revelation, and often God may also give you the interpretation and the application (the "how to") to deliver the word. Never feel pressured, however, to try to interpret a word that God isn't interpreting.

I heard a story years ago about a lady's son who needed healing. As she drove to church one night, she prayed that someone would call her out of the crowd and tell her that she had a yellow shirt on. She decided that this word would confirm to her that God had heard her prayers for her son and would heal him. That night, while the meeting was taking place, a gentleman stood up and pointed to this woman and said, "You have a yellow shirt on." The woman was not actually wearing a yellow shirt. She started weeping uncontrollably knowing that the Lord was going to heal her son.

After the man told the woman she had a yellow shirt on, he tried to interpret the meaning of the yellow shirt and continued to talk. He felt like his short word about wearing a yellow shirt must not be complete or significant enough and he kept talking. He was trying to interpret the yellow shirt when God didn't give him the interpretation.

Don't fall under this pressure! If God gives you the interpretation, be quick to give it but if He does not, let people know that you don't know what the word means. Just tell them what you are sensing from God, and let Him do the interpretation for them. When God stops talking, so should you.

Prophetic Boundaries

In order for you to prophesy safely, in ways that leave people feeling encouraged rather than hurt, I'm going to give you some prophetic boundaries. These are not meant to limit you, but rather, to keep you safe so you can practice often, which will enable you to become more accurate and comfortable with prophetic evangelism.

DON'T:

1. Don't say, "Thus says the Lord..." or "This is what the Lord says to you."

2. Thou shalt not use King James English.

3. You don't have to yell or scream while prophesying.

4. Don't prophesy dates (for example, don't give specific dates or time frames for your prophetic words).

5. Don't prophesy mates for people. It is often very dangerous and unwise to prophesy about someone's marriage status. If you have somehow misheard God, it can be emotionally and spiritually damaging to the recipient. Don't prophesy babies. I have seen many women hurt because someone carelessly prophesied that they were going to get pregnant or that they were pregnant when God did not actually say this. If a woman wants to get pregnant and she's married, it is okay for you to pray for them, but don't prophesy that God said they are going to be pregnant. Even if I feel a prophetic sense that a woman will be having a baby, rather than speaking it prophetically to her, I

just tell her, "I want to pray for you so that you can have a baby."

6. Never prophesy judgment over someone's life or reveal their sin. Your job while prophesying is to bring edification, exhortation, and comfort.

7. Don't prophesy any negative words, even if they end well (like the negative example at the beginning of this chapter).

While in public, do not act weird while prophesying. You do not need to act overly spiritual. Do not pray loudly in tongues for five minutes in front of a person at Kmart.

You don't have to try and work for a word to receive it. When you are in God's presence and experiencing His love for you and the person you are prophesying over, you can minister out of rest because you are ministering from the peace of God, not yourself.

As you operate in the gift of prophecy, understand that there is a whole new realm that is open to you that allows you to see into people's hearts and speak the very words that can change their lives forever. The Bible says that the words we speak are spirit and they are life (John 6:63). When we speak and declare what God is saying, our words shift the atmosphere around a person's life. They also impart grace, a supernatural ability for a person to step into their destiny. Prophecy is more than just words meant for the mind; our words also contain grace to empower a person to live out a prophetic word.

After you have practiced on a friend, ask them, "Does this word encourage you or make sense to you?"

There are two reasons for these questions. First, it is important to know that you are hearing from God. Second, the recipient should test the word: *"Do not quench the Spirit. Do not despise prophecies. Test all things; hold fast what is good"* (1 Thess. 5:19-21).

After practicing prophecy with your friends, go out into your community and ask the Holy Spirit to give you prophetic words for people around you. Remember, the Holy Spirit speaks many different ways. Don't be afraid to step out. Starting off, you can approach people and say something like, "Hi, my name is Chris. I'm learning to hear the voice of God. Do you mind if I pray for you right now and see what encouraging word the Lord has for you?" Everyone wants to be encouraged.

These practical steps for activation are just a brief summary to get you started. For more information on learning how to prophesy, I can highly recommend Kris Vallotton's book *Basic Training for Prophetic Ministry*, from Destiny Image Publishers.

Questions to Ponder

1. What does New Testament prophecy look like?

   _____

   _____

   _____

2. How does a prophetic gift find gold in people's lives?

   _____

   _____

   _____

3. What is the difference between a prophet and someone who prophesies?

   _____

   _____

   _____

4. Why is prophetic evangelism so effective?

   _____

   _____

   _____

Questions for Group Discussion

1. What is the fruit of negative prophecy?

   _____

   _____

2. How do prophetic boundaries help develop your gift?

_____

_____

_____

3. What would you do if you receive a prophetic word for someone but have only the revelation without interpretation?

_____

_____

_____

Life Application

Find one or more friends and practice hearing the voice of God for each other. And then ask them if the prophetic words you gave were encouraging.

Chapter 11

LEADING SUPERNATURAL EVANGELISM TEAMS

How to Get Started

God starts with our hearts. When I first started leading evangelism teams, God put a desire in my heart to see people get saved. I also had a strong desire to see others become passionate about seeing people get saved. As I grew as a leader, my leaders began to give me more opportunities to develop and lead teams.

Getting started can sometimes be the hardest part. Every believer wants to see someone get saved, but they don't know how to step out. Now that you've been equipped with the tools for supernatural evangelism, you will be empowered to be a part of evangelism teams and to possibly lead teams.

If you are already a leader in your church, get a team together and take them out. Find out what day and time works for everyone to meet and do supernatural evangelism outreaches. For an easy way to get started, I recommend Kevin Dedmon's book, *The Ultimate Treasure Hunt*.[1] A Treasure Hunt is a type of supernatural evangelism that encourages you to find the people whom God treasures in your community and to invite them into a supernatural encounter with God. Kevin calls this ministry treasure hunting because God will give you the clues (using words of knowledge) to help you find God's treasured people.

If you are a church leader, look for people around you who have a passion to get out into the community. Look for your future team leaders. As you spot your team leaders, form your core team. Spend a couple weeks with them going over this book and trying this out in your community.

When you feel your core leaders are ready to lead, you and your team leaders can open up these evangelism teams to anyone who wants to experience God move through them. You can find future team members from your own church or from other churches in your area. Connect with pastors in your area to see if you can invite members of their church to join you. Many churches may not have been trained for supernatural evangelism. From this book, you can teach people the very things that you have learned.

When your teams are ready to go out into your community, do a review of the core values before you send them out. You'll find these core values in Chapter 2.

Share past testimonies with the new people who are joining your teams, which will inspire faith and excitement to step out and take risks. Also, have your team pray for each other that everyone would have an opportunity to step out in faith and overcome fear.

After the outreach is over, do a team debrief. Ask for teams to share testimonies. Ask your teams what happened during their outreach. Ask your team to describe what they were feeling. Find out what God was doing in them, what fears they overcame, and how they plan on using today's experience to help their future ministry. Ask them, "How did today's outreach empower us to live a lifestyle of evangelism?"

If some are dealing with disappointment, encourage them. Tell people what a great job they did. If you feel they need some specific encouragement, take some time with them. After everyone leaves the outreach debrief time, people should feel encouraged.

Know Your Team

This may sound obvious, but it's very important that you get to know your team members' names. Take opportunities to get to know your team members beyond their involvement in outreach. It is in these times that you will form deeper relationships, which will build everyone up. These deep relationships will also be evident to those you are ministering to.

Encourage your teams to maintain a lifestyle of prophetic, encouraging words. Let this be evident at all times amongst your team members so that a culture of prophetic, encouraging words is created. As new people join your teams, they will naturally adapt to this culture. This way, your team members will be looking for gold in each other as well as the gold in people they meet in the community. By creating this culture in your teams, prophecy will be easy and natural rather than a special event that occurs only occasionally. Prophecy will flow naturally during the outreach. Forming outreach teams and going into your community on special outreach days trains believers to live a lifestyle of supernatural evangelism. Evangelism should not be confined to a special day, but practicing with fellow believers builds confidence and encourages people to make this a regular part of their lives.

A new commandment I give to you, that you love one another; as I have loved you, that you also love one another. By this all will know that you are My disciples, if you have love for one another (John 13:34-35).

As you are leading your team, you'll notice different people who have different strengths. As a leader, always encourage the strengths you see in them. If one person excels in a certain area, encourage the other team members to recognize their strengths as well.

Know Your City

As a leader, you can either have a vision to have a testimony or you can have a vision to see your city transformed. When we talk about transformation, we are talking about people who live in certain areas in your community. In Redding, California, we have purposed to know our city and the people who live here. Because of consistent, intentional relationships through life and outreaches, our city is being transformed.

When you pray for your city, where does the Holy Spirit lead you? Go wherever the Holy Spirit leads you and invest your life and your resources in that area. Often when the Holy Spirit highlights certain areas, it's because He wants to give you influence and authority there. In God's heart, there are areas in each city and nation that He is highlighting to us in this season. Yes, it is true that He wants everyone saved, but there are certain locations that God has strategic plans for.

Maybe God is calling you to plant a church in a certain location of your city. Maybe the church you are planting is in your neighborhood. Maybe the church is in the house of a person the Holy Spirit has told you to go to and befriend. You never know what can happen until you step out and be obedient to the Holy Spirit.

Ask the Holy Spirit, "Where do You want me, as a leader, to invest in? Where should we send our teams? Should we send them everywhere or just to key locations?"

When the Holy Spirit tells you where to invest yourself and your team, write that area down. Begin to pray, "Holy Spirit, show me more! What do You want me to do in this area?" Wait for the Holy Spirit to give you the blueprints.

When God places a fire in your heart to touch your city, you know that when you pray, God is going to speak to you and He is going to reveal to you the blueprints and the master plan that is in Heaven for your city.

Building Up Your Team in Love

Years ago, I took a team to South Africa. One of the pastors we worked with said, "Chris, we have a lot of teams that come through here. We've seen a lot of miracles take place. But we rarely ever see teams that really love each other like you guys do. The people that you are sharing with, they are talking about how you guys love each other. This is the greatest thing we have seen from all the teams we have had out here."

There are all kinds of activities you can do to build up a team. The greatest thing you can do is to teach your team how to love. They will learn this from your example.

Authentic love starts in our heart when we experience God's love, which empowers us to love each other, and then love the world around us.

Each team member needs to feel like their life is valuable and significant; that their life makes a difference on the team.

> You, as a leader, can build up your team by speaking God's love and encouragement to them. Live your life on display so that you are an example to your team.

You, as a leader, can build up your team by speaking God's love and encouragement to them. Live your life on display so that you are an example to your team. Encourage them often. Build them up with words of love. Speak into their destiny and their inner potential to become a great leader.

Weed out jealousy and competition with love. Do not allow it to have any place on your team. You do that by being an encourager. Teach others to look for the gold in their own lives and the lives of their teammates. Listen to their stories. Rejoice with them in their breakthrough, because their breakthrough becomes a blessing to the whole team.

As a team leader, remember that your team is more than just an outreach team. It is a team of people whom God has placed in your life. These relationships that God has given you will last longer than just an outreach. Make time to hang out together outside of ministry. This will let you and your team get to know each other, learn to love each other, and become a family bonded in love.

Freely Receive, Freely Give

The more we receive, the more we have an opportunity to give away what we have received. This enables us to receive more as well. I hope this book has helped to spark a fire in your spirit to touch the world around you with the love and power of God. Whatever you have received through faith, give that freely away, and you will freely receive more. The world that we live in is in desperate need for you to become everything you have been created to be. When you shine your light, the darkness has to flee!

Questions to Ponder

1. How does having the core values mentioned in Chapter 2 empower you as a leader of supernatural evangelism teams?

   _____

   _____

   _____

2. As a leader, why should love be one of the main motivators that your teams should minister from?

   _____

   _____

   _____

3. How does creating a safe atmosphere of risk empower people to step into new realms?

   _____

   _____

   _____

4. As a leader, why is it important that you see the greatness in people you are leading?

   _____

   _____

   _____

Questions for Group Discussion

1. What are some of the needs you see in your community that you can possibly fill?

   _____

   _____

   _____

2. How does love empower a team to be more effective?

   _____

   _____

   _____

Life Application

As a leader, look for people who you can teach based on this book and who can then be on your team as you go out into the community and put into practice what you've learned.

Endnote

1. Kevin Dedmon, *The Ultimate Treasure Hunt: The Ultimate Guide to Supernatural Evangelism Through Supernatural Encounters* (Shippensburg, PA: Destiny Image Publishers, 2007).

Appendix A

SALVATION SCRIPTURES

For all have sinned, and come short of the glory of God (Romans 3:23 KJV).

For the wages of sin is death; but the gift of God is eternal life through Jesus Christ our Lord (Romans 6:23).

But as many as received Him, to them gave He power to become the sons of God, even to them that believe on His name (John 1:12 KJV).

Behold, I stand at the door, and knock: if any man hear My voice, and open the door, I will come in to him, and will sup with him, and he with Me (Revelation 3:20 KJV).

And this is the record, that God hath given to us eternal life, and this life is in His Son. He that hath the Son hath life; and he that hath not the Son of God hath not life. These things have I written unto you that believe on the name of the Son of God; that ye may know that ye have eternal life, and that ye may believe on the name of the Son of God (1 John 5:11-13 KJV).

If we confess our sins, He is faithful and just to forgive us our sins, and to cleanse us from all unrighteousness (1 John 1:9 KJV).

For by grace are ye saved through faith; and that not of yourselves: it is the gift of God: not of works, lest any man should boast (Ephesians 2:8-9 KJV).

Therefore if any man be in Christ, he is a new creature: old things are passed away; behold, all things are become new (2 Corinthians 5:17 KJV).

That if thou shalt confess with thy mouth the Lord Jesus, and shalt believe in thine heart that God hath raised Him from the dead, thou shalt be saved. For with the heart man believeth unto righteousness; and with the mouth confession is made unto salvation (Romans 10:9-10 KJV).

For God so loved the world, that He gave His only begotten Son, that whosoever believeth in Him should not perish, but have everlasting life. For God sent not His Son into the world to condemn the world; but that the world through Him might be saved (John 3:16-17 KJV).

And this is life eternal, that they might know Thee the only true God, and Jesus Christ, whom Thou hast sent (John 17:3 KJV).

All we like sheep have gone astray; we have turned every one to his own way; and the Lord hath laid on Him the iniquity of us all (Isaiah 53:6 KJV).

And as it is appointed unto men once to die, but after this the judgment (Hebrews 9:27 KJV).

But God commendeth His love toward us, in that, while we were yet sinners, Christ died for us (Romans 5:8 KJV).

Therefore we are buried with Him by baptism into death: that like as Christ was raised up from the dead by the glory of the Father, even so we also should walk in newness of life (Romans 6:4 KJV).

For Christ also hath once suffered for sins, the just for the unjust, that He might bring us to God, being put to death in the flesh, but quickened by the Spirit (1 Peter 3:18 KJV).

And saying, The time is fulfilled, and the kingdom of God is at hand: repent ye, and believe the gospel (Mark 1:15 KJV).

As far as the east is from the west, so far hath He removed our transgressions from us (Psalm 103:12 KJV).

We love Him, because He first loved us (1 John 4:19 KJV).

If the Son therefore shall make you free, ye shall be free indeed (John 8:36 KJV).

And again I say unto you, It is easier for a camel to go through the eye of a needle, than for a rich man to enter into the kingdom of God. When His disciples heard it, they were exceedingly amazed, saying, Who then can be saved? But Jesus beheld them, and said unto them, With men this is impossible; but with God all things are possible (Matthew 19:24-26 KJV).

But he that shall endure unto the end, the same shall be saved (Matthew 24:13 KJV).

He that believeth and is baptized shall be saved; but he that believeth not shall be damned (Mark 16:16 KJV).

And He said to the woman, Thy faith hath saved thee; go in peace (Luke 7:50 KJV).

Those by the way side are they that hear; then cometh the devil, and taketh away the word out of their hearts, lest they should believe and be saved (Luke 8:12 KJV).

But I receive not testimony from man: but these things I say, that ye might be saved (John 5:34 KJV).

I am the door: by Me if any man enter in, he shall be saved, and shall go in and out, and find pasture (John 10:9 KJV).

And it shall come to pass, that whosoever shall call on the name of the Lord shall be saved... (Acts 2:21 KJV).

But we believe that through the grace of the Lord Jesus Christ we shall be saved (Acts 15:11 KJV).

And brought them out, and said, Sirs, what must I do to be saved? And they said, Believe on the Lord Jesus Christ, and thou shalt be saved, and thy house (Acts 16:30-31 KJV).

Praising God, and having favour with all the people. And the Lord added to the church daily such as should be saved (Acts 2:47 KJV).

Neither is there salvation in any other: for there is none other name under heaven given among men, whereby we must be saved (Acts 4:12 KJV).

Much more then, being now justified by His blood, we shall be saved from wrath through Him. For if, when we were enemies, we were reconciled to God by the death of His Son, much more, being reconciled, we shall be saved by His life (Romans 5:9-10 KJV).

Not by works of righteousness which we have done, but according to His mercy He saved us, by the washing of regeneration, and renewing of the Holy Ghost (Titus 3:5 KJV).

For whosoever shall call upon the name of the Lord shall be saved (Romans 10:13 KJV).

HEALING SCRIPTURES

"...If you diligently heed the voice of the Lord your God and do what is right in His sight, give ear to His commandments and keep all His statutes, I will put none of the diseases on you which I have brought on the Egyptians. For I am the Lord who heals you" (Exodus 15:26).

So you shall serve the Lord your God, and He will bless your bread and your water. And I will take sickness away from the midst of you (Exodus 23:25).

Blessed be the Lord, who has given rest to His people Israel, according to all that He promised. There has not failed one word of all His good promise, which He promised through His servant Moses (1 Kings 8:56).

Bless the Lord, O my soul; and all that is within me, bless His holy name! Bless the Lord, O my soul, and forget not all His benefits: who forgives all your iniquities, who heals all your diseases, who redeems your life from destruction, who crowns you with lovingkindness and tender mercies, who satisfies your mouth with good things, so that your youth is renewed like the eagle's (Psalm 103:1-5).

He sent His word and healed them, and delivered them from their destructions (Psalm 107:20).

I shall not die, but live, and declare the works of the Lord (Psalm 118:17).

My son, give attention to my words; incline your ear to my sayings. Do not let them depart from your eyes; keep them in the midst of your heart; for they are life to those who find them, and health to all their flesh. Keep your heart with all diligence, for out of it spring the issues of life (Proverbs 4:20-23).

Pleasant words are like a honeycomb, sweetness to the soul and health to the bones (Proverbs 16:24).

A merry heart does good, like medicine, but a broken spirit dries the bones (Proverbs 17:22).

He was wounded for our transgressions, He was bruised for our iniquities; the chastisement of our peace was upon Him, and by His stripes we are healed (Isaiah 53:5).

As for the days of our life, they contain seventy years or if due to strength, eighty years (Psalm 90:10 NASB).

With a long life I will satisfy him (Psalm 91:16).

Surely our griefs [sicknesses] He Himself bore, and our sorrows [pain] He carried; yet we ourselves esteemed Him stricken, smitten of God, and afflicted (Isaiah 53:4 NASB).

This was to fulfill what was spoken through Isaiah the prophet: "He Himself took our infirmities and carried away our diseases" (Matthew 8:17 NASB).

He Himself bore our sins in His body on the cross, so that we might die to sin and live to righteousness;: for by His wounds you were healed (1 Peter 2:24 NASB).

But if the Spirit of Him who raised Jesus from the dead dwells in you, He who raised Christ from the dead will also give life to your mortal bodies through His Spirit who dwells in you (Romans 8:11 NASB).

That He would grant you, according to the riches of His glory, to be strengthened with power through His Spirit in the inner man (Ephesians 3:16 NASB).

Now to Him who is able to do far more abundantly beyond all that we ask or think, according to the power that works within us (Ephesians 3:20 NASB).

Now may the God of hope fill you with all joy and peace in believing, that you may abound in hope by the power of the Holy Spirit (Romans 15:13).

If you remain in Me and My words remain in you, ask whatever you wish, and it will be given you (John 15:7 NIV).

For I will restore health to you and heal you of your wounds... (Jeremiah 30:17).

Ah, Lord God! Behold, You have made the heavens and the earth by Your great power and outstretched arm. There is nothing too hard for You (Jeremiah 32:17).

Then Jesus went about all the cities and villages, teaching in their synagogues, preaching the gospel of the kingdom, and healing every sickness and disease among the people (Matthew 9:35).

And Jesus went forth, and saw a great multitude, and was moved with compassion toward them, and He healed their sick (Matthew 14:14 KJV).

I tell you the truth, if you have faith as small as a mustard seed, you can say to this mountain, "Move from here to there" and it will move. Nothing will be impossible for you (Matthew 17:20 NIV).

Jesus replied, "I tell you the truth, if you have faith and do not doubt, not only can you do what was done to the fig tree, but also you can say to this mountain, 'Go throw yourself into the sea,' and it will be done. If you believe, you will receive whatever you ask for in prayer" (Matthew 21:21-22 NIV).

Therefore I say to you, whatever things you ask when you pray, believe that you receive them, and you will have them (Mark 11:24).

When the sun was setting, all those who had any that were sick with various disease brought them to Him; and He laid His hands on every one of them and healed them (Luke 4:40).

The thief does not come except to steal, and to kill, and to destroy. I have come that they may have life, and that you may have it more abundantly (John 10:10).

I tell you the truth, anyone who has faith in Me will do what I have been doing. He will do even greater things than these, because I am going to the Father. And I will do whatever you ask in My name, so that the Son may bring glory to the Father. You may ask Me for anything in My name, and I will do it (John 14:12-14 NIV).

Be anxious for nothing, but in everything by prayer and supplication, with thanksgiving, let your requests be made known to God; and the peace of God, which surpasses all understanding, will guard your hearts and minds through Christ Jesus (Philippians 4:6-7).

I can do all things through Christ who strengthens me (Philippians 4:13).

And my God will meet all your needs according to His glorious riches in Christ Jesus (Philippians 4:19 NIV).

Behold, I have given you authority to tread on serpents and scorpions, and over all the power of the enemy, and nothing will injure you (Luke 10:19 NASB).

This is the confidence we have in approaching God: that if we ask anything according to His will, He hears us. And if we know that He hears us—whatever we ask—we know that we have what we asked of Him (1 John 5:14-15 NIV).

Beloved, I pray that you may prosper in all things and be in health, just as your soul prospers (3 John 2).

YOUR TESTIMONIES

Date: ___ / ___ / ___ Word Given To: _____

Testimony: _____

_____

_____

_____

_____

_____

_____

Date: ___ / ___ / ___ Word Given To: _____

Testimony: _____

_____

_____

_____

_____

_____

_____

Date: ___ / ___ / ___ Word Given To: _____

Testimony: _____

_____

_____

_____

_____

_____

_____

_____

_____

Date: ___ / ___ / ___ Word Given To: _____

Testimony: _____

_____

_____

_____

_____

_____

_____

_____

_____

Date: ___ / ___ / ___ Word Given To: _____

Testimony: _____

_____

_____

_____

_____

_____

_____

_____

_____

Date: ___ / ___ / ___ Word Given To: _____

Testimony: _____

_____

_____

_____

_____

_____

_____

_____

_____

Date: ___ / ___ / ___ Word Given To: _____

Testimony: _____

_____

_____

_____

_____

_____

_____

_____

_____

_____

Date: ___ / ___ / ___ Word Given To: _____

Testimony: _____

_____

_____

_____

_____

_____

_____

_____

_____

_____

Date: ___ / ___ / ___ Word Given To: _____

Testimony: _____

_____

_____

_____

_____

_____

_____

_____

_____

Date: ___ / ___ / ___ Word Given To: _____

Testimony: _____

_____

_____

_____

_____

_____

_____

_____

_____

Date: ___ / ___ / ___ Word Given To: _____

Testimony: _____

_____

_____

_____

_____

_____

_____

_____

_____

Date: ___ / ___ / ___ Word Given To: _____

Testimony: _____

_____

_____

_____

_____

_____

_____

_____

_____

PROPHETIC WORDS

Date: ___ / ___ / ___ Word Given To: _____

Prophecy: _____

_____

_____

_____

_____

_____

_____

Date: ___ / ___ / ___ Word Given To: _____

Prophecy: _____

_____

_____

_____

_____

_____

_____

Date: ___ / ___ / ___ Word Given To: _____

Prophecy: _____

_____

_____

_____

_____

_____

_____

_____

_____

_____

Date: ___ / ___ / ___ Word Given To: _____

Prophecy: _____

_____

_____

_____

_____

_____

_____

_____

_____

Date: ___ / ___ / ___ Word Given To: _____

Prophecy: _____

_____

_____

_____

_____

_____

_____

_____

_____

_____

Date: ___ / ___ / ___ Word Given To: _____

Prophecy: _____

_____

_____

_____

_____

_____

_____

_____

_____

_____

Date: __ / __ / __ Word Given To: _____

Prophecy: _____

_____

_____

_____

_____

_____

_____

_____

_____

Date: __ / __ / __ Word Given To: _____

Prophecy: _____

_____

_____

_____

_____

_____

_____

_____

Date: ___ / ___ / ___ Word Given To: _____

Prophecy: _____

_____

_____

_____

_____

_____

_____

_____

_____

_____

Date: ___ / ___ / ___ Word Given To: _____

Prophecy: _____

_____

_____

_____

_____

_____

_____

_____

_____

About Chris Overstreet

Chris Overstreet is the Outreach Pastor at Bethel Church in Redding California. He has had the privilege of training and equipping thousands of students who have attended the School of Supernatural Ministry in Evangelism at Bethel Church. He trained them to live a lifestyle of miracles, signs, and wonders while demonstrating the love and power of God in their community. Chris also oversees the active outreach ministry at Bethel Church and is the director of the Bethel School of Supernatural Evangelism, which hosts many schools in Redding and in other cities around the world. Chris and his wife Stefanie travel within the USA and abroad with the vision to see believers equipped for the end-time harvest of the age.

Chris Overstreet, contact information

Chris Overstreet
Outreach Pastor of Bethel Church, Redding, CA
www.ibethel.org
530-246-6000

Resources

Bethel School of Supernatural Evangelism, filmed in Anderson, CA Feb. 2010. DVD set and CD school set available through www.ibethel.org/store

BETHEL SCHOOL OF SUPERNATURAL EVANGELISM

The Bethel School of Supernatural Evangelism will equip and empower both the seasoned and most timid believer to demonstrate the Kingdom of Heaven through love and power. If you hunger to see God move through you to display real power that touches lives with His love, you don't want to miss this school.

Bethel School of Supernatural Evangelism is a school that will equip you to have a Kingdom mindset that empowers ordinary people to openly display the raw power of God in your own community. In this school, you will be trained and equipped by many of Bethel's leaders who will help you develop a supernatural lifestyle of miracles, signs and wonders, salvation encounters, and deliverances. If you are a leader or individual who desires to move in the supernatural outside the four walls of the church, this school is for you. People have been transformed as a result of this training and equipping, and empowered to live their lives naturally supernatural.

In the right hands, This Book will Change Lives!

Most of the people who need this message will not be looking for this book. To change their lives, you need to put a copy of this book in their hands.

> *But others (seeds) fell into good ground, and brought forth fruit, some a hundred-fold, some sixty-fold, some thirty-fold* (Matthew 13:8).

Our ministry is constantly seeking methods to find the good ground, the people who need this anointed message to change their lives. Will you help us reach these people?

> *Remember this—a farmer who plants only a few seeds will get a small crop. But the one who plants generously will get a generous crop* (2 Corinthians 9:6).

EXTEND THIS MINISTRY BY SOWING
3 BOOKS, 5 BOOKS, 10 BOOKS, OR MORE TODAY,
AND BECOME A LIFE CHANGER!

Thank you,

Don Nori Sr., Publisher
Destiny Image
Since 1982

DESTINY IMAGE PUBLISHERS, INC.

*"Speaking to the Purposes of God for This Generation
and for the Generations to Come."*

VISIT OUR NEW SITE HOME AT
WWW.DESTINYIMAGE.COM

FREE SUBSCRIPTION TO DI NEWSLETTER

Receive free unpublished articles by top DI authors, exclusive

discounts, and free downloads from our best and newest books.

Visit www.destinyimage.com to subscribe.

Write to: Destiny Image
              P.O. Box 310
              Shippensburg, PA 17257-0310

Call: 1-800-722-6774

Email: orders@destinyimage.com

For a complete list of our titles or to place an order
online, visit www.destinyimage.com.

FIND US ON FACEBOOK OR FOLLOW US ON TWITTER.

www.facebook.com/destinyimage   facebook
www.twitter.com/destinyimage   twitter